BERNARD OF CLAIRVAUX

Volume One

TREATISES I

CISTERCIAN FATHERS SERIES

CISTERCIAN FATHERS SERIES : NUMBER ONE

THE WORKS OF
BERNARD OF CLAIRVAUX

Volume One

Treatises I

CISTERCIAN PUBLICATIONS

Spencer, Massachusetts

1970

The translation here presented is based on the critical Latin edition prepared by Jean Leclercq OSB and Henri Rochais OSB under the sponsorship of the S. Order of Cistercians and published by Editiones Cistercienses, Piazza Tempio di Diana, 14-1-00153, Rome, Italy.

Ecclesiastical permission to publish this book was received from Bernard Flanagan, Bishop of Worcester, April 23rd, 1969.

Printed in the Republic of Ireland by
Cahill & Co. Limited, Parkgate Printing Works, Dublin

DEDICATION

One of the first General Chapters of the Order of Cîteaux determined that all the monasteries of the Order should be dedicated to the Blessed Virgin Mary. And so should all the work that is done in these monasteries. Therefore,

to

MARY

the Mother of Cîteaux

we dedicate the

CISTERCIAN FATHERS SERIES.

CONTENTS

Contents

THE OFFICE OF ST VICTOR

EDITOR'S NOTE

With this volume the reader is introduced to the Cɪsᴛᴇʀᴄɪᴀɴ
Fᴀᴛʜᴇʀs Sᴇʀɪᴇs. This series is sponsored by the Cistercian communities of America primarily to provide Cistercian monks and nuns
with good English translations of the Fathers of the Order. A
qualified team of translators under the direction of an international
Board of Editors, including some of the most outstanding monastic
scholars of our times, will work from the recently established critical
editions. The translations will be accompanied by introductions,
notes and indexes prepared by competent scholars. It is hoped that
these translations will also serve others—religious, scholars and the
concerned layman.

We have chosen for our first volume four short works of the
best known Cistercian, Bernard of Clairvaux. These particular
works have been chosen because, unlike most of the other works of
St Bernard, they have never before to our knowledge been published
in English. Moreover, they have a very special relevance to the
present time when we are intent upon monastic renewal. Renewal
in its fullest sense was one of the basic thrusts of the Cistercian
spirit. In these works we find the "Theologian of the Cistercian
Life" bringing this force into confrontation with the existing monastic order. While some of the more eloquent exaggeration of
Bernard's *Apologia* is fairly well known, not so well known is the
overall context of humble frankness and fraternal love.

This *Apologia* provoked by the great Benedictine of the times, and written for another Benedictine at his insistence, is very appropriately introduced here by one of the outstanding Benedictine scholars of our times who helps us to see it in its full context.

While Bernard's book *On Precept and Dispensation* was written as a response to particular questions, it does give him occasion to expose some fundamental attitudes toward a monastic life according to the Rule of St Benedict. In doing this he touches on not a few of the crucial questions that we are struggling with in our renewal efforts: interpretation of the Rule, abbatial authority, local stability.

Finally, in his *Prologue* for the revised Cistercian Antiphonary, Bernard is with us in our struggle to renew the liturgy. However, the only authentic example that has come down to us of his own personal effort to implement the principles which he has enunciated is the brief *Office of St Victor* which is included here for this reason.

While the publication of these translations has a particular relevance to present concern, it is hoped that they will have a lasting value, for renewal must be a constant ongoing process.

We will be grateful to receive from our readers any suggestions which will help us make the succeeding volumes of the CISTERCIAN FATHERS SERIES more satisfactory.

M. Basil Pennington ocso

CISTERCIANS AND CLUNIACS

ST BERNARD'S
APOLOGIA TO ABBOT WILLIAM

INTRODUCTION

THE APOLOGIA was written in 1125, when St Bernard was thirty-five years old. He had been a Cistercian monk for twelve years, and abbot of Clairvaux for ten. We know that by this time both his literary talents and his spiritual outlook were fully developed. He had already written some of his letters, as well as the first redaction of his homilies *In Praise of the Virgin Mary*[1] and about the same time he was also engaged in the composition of *The Steps of Humility*.[2] Neither of these two treatises was polemic in character, so that the *Apologia* was a step in a new direction.

This tract was a product of the controversy which arose between the Cistercians and the adherents of an established monasticism, regarding the interpretation of the Rule of St Benedict. In the older monasteries—the ones we today would call "Benedictine," and whose members were known in those days from the color of their habits as "Black Monks"—a long process of development had brought about a situation in which the life of the monks was moderated, not only by the Rule, but also by a set of customs based on the ecclesiastical, liturgical, economic, sociological and psychological conditions of a former age. In contrast stood the Cistercians. Like all the new orders that made their appearance about this time, they wished to live more simply and poorly, and their habit of

1. Cf. *S. Bernardi Opera* (Rome: Editiones Cistercienses, 1966), IV, p. 3.
2. *Ibid.*, III (1963), pp. 3f.

3

plain undyed wool was a symbol of this aspiration. The "Grey Monks," as they were called, wanted to live according to the Rule of St Benedict, to return to the basic pattern of Benedictine life which had, they thought, been obscured and obstructed by the customs that had accumulated over the years. The founders of such orders had no desire to reform the existing system of monasticism, as if to suggest that it was completely degenerate. Their aim was to establish a new form of monastic life, one that would be closer to the Rule, and at the same time, more in harmony with the contemporary situation.[3]

The reaction of the Black Monks was instinctive; they felt slighted and lost no time in defending themselves. Meanwhile, some of the Cistercians, rightly proud of their Order, were becoming self-satisfied and critical of the Black Monks. Of course not all monks were involved, but the difference of opinion was sufficiently stimulating to provoke, within the space of a hundred years or so, no less than eleven tracts, which trace out for us the development of monastic thought during this period.[4] Of these the most famous is St Bernard's *Apologia*.

Origin of the Apologia

We are fortunate in having fairly detailed knowledge of the circumstances surrounding the composition of the *Apologia*. It may be worthwhile to recall them briefly, since this gives us an opportunity of seeing St Bernard at work, slowly bringing a book to completion. In the present case the process lasted at least six months.

3. I have tried to show this in my article "The Intention of the Founders of the Cistercian Order" in *The Cistercian Spirit: A Symposium* (Cistercian Studies Series, 3).

4. A list of these tracts will be found in the bibliography. They are analyzed by A. Wilmart in "Une riposte de l'ancien monachisme au manifeste de S. Bernard" in *Revue bénédictine*, 46 (1934), pp. 296–305. Some of the sociological aspects of the controversy are treated by A. H. Bredero in "The Controversy between Peter the Venerable and Saint Bernard of Clairvaux" in *Petrus Venerabilis, 1156-1956*, pp. 53–71.

Lent in 1125 extended from February 11 to March 28. In the course of it Bernard wrote to Oger, a Canon Regular of Mont-Saint-Eloi in the diocese of Arras. He referred to his booklet *The Steps of Humility*, and to his homilies *In Praise of the Virgin Mary*.[5] About the same time, during the spring, he wrote the famous letter to his cousin Robert, reproaching him for leaving the Cistercians and going to Cluny. On this occasion Bernard compared the two ways of life in a manner which was entirely on the side of Cîteaux, and very critical of Cluny.[6] He states explicitly in this letter, that until then he had done nothing at which Cluniacs might take exception,[7] but from the time the contents of the letter became known he would be accused of slandering Cluny. In a letter written to Simon, abbot of Saint-Nicholas-aux-Bois, explaining why he had refused to accept a monk of this monastery into Clairvaux,[8] he demonstrated his good will toward the Order. Later, when Bernard came to write his *Apologia*, he will recall this fact.[9]

It was about this time, spring or perhaps the start of summer, that Bernard received a communication from William, abbot of St Thierry in the diocese of Rheims. The letter itself is no longer extant, but we do have Bernard's reply:

I am quite prepared to undertake the task you have enjoined on me for the removal of scandal from God's kingdom, but at the moment I cannot quite see how you would like it done. I have read and reread your beautiful letter—with ever more enjoyment, since it does not pall with repetition—and I understand that you want me to convince those who complain that we are slandering the Order of Cluny, that the malicious tale which they believe and spread abroad is not true. However, it

5. *Letter* 89, 3; PL 182:221; trans. B. S. James, *The Letters of St. Bernard of Clairvaux* (London: Burns & Oates, 1953), no. 92, p. 138. Cf. *S. Bernardi Opera*, III, p. 4.

6. See D. van den Eynde, "Les premiers écrits de S. Bernard" in Leclercq, *Recueil d'études sur saint Bernard et ses écrits* (Rome: Edizioni di Storia e Letteratura, 1968), III, pp. 396ff.

7. *Letter* 1, 11; PL 182:76; trans. James, no. 1, p. 7.

8. *Letter* 84; PL 182:205; trans. James, no. 86, p. 124.

9. *Infra*, no. 4.

seems contradictory to me, having done just this, to turn round and condemn their excesses in food and clothing and the other areas you mention. Perhaps I could say first that the Order itself is quite praiseworthy, and that those who censure it should themselves be censured, and then go on to condemn the excesses present in it. Tell me frankly if this is what you want, or whether you think a different approach is called for. Do not hesitate to tell me what you want, and I shall do it. At the same time you should be aware that I find this sort of writing rather distasteful. It means a great loss of devotion and an interruption of prayer, especially when one has neither the skill nor the leisure for writing.[10]

Some have thought that this letter forms a preface to the *Apologia*, but this is not so. The letter is interesting though, because like Bernard's prefaces, it offers us a glimpse into the mind of its author. It informs us that Bernard is writing at William's request, or rather on his orders, and that its purpose is the serious one of putting an end to a scandal in God's kingdom. The charge that the Cistercians were slandering Cluny must be refuted, and the laxity which had become accepted at Cluny must be denounced. Bernard agreed that such a work was desirable. He knew also that he had something to say on this matter and that he had the prestige and competence to do so. At the same time he could not quite see how such a task could be done without making matters worse, or without contradicting himself. Could he praise the Cluniacs first, and then denounce them? His dilemma was not merely on the literary plane; religious and moral values also were involved. To solve this problem Bernard asks prayers and clarification. He himself would rather have written nothing, since he was a busy man, and he preferred to spend in prayer whatever leisure he had. We have no grounds for doubting the sincerity of this reluctance; it is in fact to the credit of this great monk.

William's reply must have smoothed matters out, for Bernard set about writing the tract. He dedicated it to William, since it was at his command that he was writing. He explained to his readers

---

10. *Letter* 84bis, *S. Bernardi Opera*, III, p. 64.

how the seriousness of the situation had overcome his natural repugnance for the task, and how he found himself with no alternative but to take up the pen and write as best he could. It was distasteful for him since it was no business of the monk to set himself up as judge. Jerome had written in this respect: "From our holes in the ground and our cells, we pass judgment on the world."[11] Bernard knew that he would be the object of the same sort of sarcasm if he did not do something about it. He alludes to the passage—but without mentioning Jerome by name—in the hope that alert readers might catch the reminiscence and realize that the paradox had not escaped his attention. He then outlines the scope of the tract, saying nothing, however, about his attitude to Cluny's shortcomings. In this way he tries to soften up the Black Monks. It is not very difficult to imagine their glee on a first reading, to find their adversaries so convincingly rebuked.

Then Bernard got down to work, and sometime in the summer he was able to send Oger a rough draft. Oger acknowledged receiving it, and wrote that he had compiled a preface from some of Bernard's letters, and that he had made a copy of the draft and sent it to William of St Thierry.[12] Bernard replied that this was not quite what he had intended; at the same time he admitted that he did not mind, since William was such a close friend. The text of Bernard's letter runs as follows:

That other booklet I lent you, I had meant you only to read, but you tell me that you have had it copied. What use that can serve or whom it can possibly benefit is your responsibility. I did not intend that you should send it to the abbot of St Thierry, but I do not mind. Why should I mind his seeing it when I would gladly lay bare my whole soul for him to see if I could. . . . Do not hesitate, I beg you, to find an opportunity of going to see him, and do not, on any account, allow anyone to see or copy the aforesaid booklet until you have been through it with him, discussed it with him, and have both made such corrections as

11. Jerome, *Letter* 17, 2; C.S.E.L. 64, p. 71; trans. W. H. Fremantle, *Nicene and Post-Nicene Fathers*, second series, vol. VI, p. 21.
12. Van den Eynde, *op. cit.*, p. 399.

B

may be necessary that every word of it may be supported by two witnesses. I leave to you both to decide whether the preface you have put together out of my other letters will stand, or whether it would not be better to compose another.[13]

The following facts can be deduced from this letter: 1) Bernard had sent Oger a draft of the *Apologia* to read, but not to copy. 2) Oger had made a copy of it on his own initiative, and sent it to William of St Thierry. 3) Bernard did not disapprove of this. 4) He asked Oger to go over the text thoroughly with William, to discuss it and amend it, and to decide whether the brief preface (*praefatiuncula*) Oger had compiled was suitable, or whether something else was called for.

This raises both literary and psychological problems. In the first place, why did Bernard not send the draft to his friend, at whose instigation he was writing the *Apologia*, instead of to Oger with whom he was, to say the least, on much less familiar terms?

The answer can be found at the psychological level. It may be inferred from Bernard's letter to William that the abbot of Clairvaux was worried about the outcome of his intervention, and afraid of the reactions it might provoke. Accordingly, it is possible that he thought it a wise plan to submit the text to someone before publishing it, someone who was quite sympathetic to him, yet not so involved as William in the Cistercian-Cluniac controversy.

Is the text Bernard sent to Oger extant? There is no sign of it among the manuscripts; nor is this surprising, inasmuch as it was only a preliminary draft, not intended for publication.

Toward the end of the tract Bernard apologizes for having to bring his remarks to a precipitate conclusion: "I am prevented from going on by the burdens of my office, and by your imminent departure, dear brother Oger. You will not agree to stay any longer, and you refuse to go without this latest little book."[14] This quotation together with its context are part of the definitive text of the *Apologia*, but it was absent from the draft Bernard sent to

---

13. *Letter* 88, 3; PL 182:213; trans. James, no. 91, pp. 136f.
14. *Infra*, no. 30.

Oger, and Oger had transmitted to William. Letter eighty-eight was written after this had happened. At that stage Oger had not yet paid his visit to Clairvaux, and Bernard was not sure whether he was coming at all. It is impossible, therefore, that the draft sent to Oger includes this passage which implies that Oger was at Clairvaux for the writing of the definitive text.

Having listened to the comments of Oger and William, Bernard brings the first edition of the *Apologia* to an end. This, however, is not the conclusion of its textual development. During the summer, William asked Bernard to send him a brief preface, *praefatiuncula*, since the *Apologia* did not have one. Bernard replied that he had considered it unnecessary and had not written one.[15]

Manuscript evidence shows that the *Apologia* underwent further revision after the publication of the first edition. It is possible that William of St Thierry had offered some further suggestions on how to improve the text, as he did in the case of Bernard's tract against Abelard.[16] This first edition can be distinguished from the definitive edition by the following characteristics:

1) In chapter eight a long passage running from "For this kind of mercy . . ." in number sixteen to the beginning of number eighteen is not included.

2) In chapter nine there is a significant modification of a few phrases in number twenty-one.

3) Again in chapter nine, the whole of number twenty-two and some of number twenty-three are absent.

4) There are more than sixty variant readings of no great importance, beginning with *si quid* and *non ut*, instead of *si qua* and *non quia*, in the opening lines, and continuing through to the omission of *Deo auctore* and *ipso protectore* toward the end.

5) There are no section divisions, either by paragraph headings or by rubrics inserted in the text itself.

---

15. *Letter* 85, 4; PL 182:209; trans. James, no. 87, p. 127.

16. I have tried to show this in two articles: "Les formes successives de la lettre-traité de s. Bernard contre Abélard" in *Revue bénédictine*, 78 (1968), pp. 87–105, and "Les lettres de Guillaume de Saint-Thierry," which will be published in *Revue bénédictine*, 79 (1969).

Taken collectively, these variants point to a primitive edition of the text of the *Apologia* which was shorter and less polished than the one we have. The idea of the second edition was not to correct the first, as though it were faulty, but to improve it and to sharpen the nuances of its formulas. An example of this can be found in number twenty-one, where a phrase is eliminated which refers to the fact that Bernard himself had seen the abuses he was describing in the refectory at Cluny. An equivalent phrase, added in number twenty-two is very much milder. On the other hand, the two long insertions mentioned above serve only to reinforce the theme the *Apologia* has been developing all the while. These changes are much the same as those found in the two authentic editions of the sermons *On the Song of Songs*,[17] and the sermons on Psalm 90.[18]

All the variant readings proper to the first edition are itemized in the apparatus of the critical edition of the text. Here it is sufficient to say that there are not many manuscripts that follow the primitive version. This can be explained by the fact that it was only provisional, and would shortly be replaced by the definitive text. The copies we have could derive either from the original that Bernard gave to Oger, or from a copy William had at St Thierry, and which went with him to Signy. It is fairly probable that we do not possess all the copies that were made of the primitive version, though, judging from the ones we have, it seems that it never enjoyed a very wide circulation. All the ancient manuscripts which follow it, as well as the later ones with the exception of the one from Echarlis are to be found in the north of France, round the area where William and Oger had lived. Oger was a canon of Mont-Saint-Eloi in the diocese of Arras, but in 1125 he became abbot of St Médard at Tournai. The text crossed into England by way of Fécamp, which is in the diocese of Rouen, not far from Arras. Steinfeld is near Bonn, but between 1121 and 1135 this house of canons regular of the Springiersbach observance was attached by Evervin to the abbey of Prémontré, which was in the diocese of Laon, not far from Signy and St Thierry, and from which

17. Cf. *Recueil*, I (1962), pp. 329ff.
18. *Ibid.*, vol. III.

Steinfeld could easily have received its copy. Oger himself was a canon regular, and according to Vacandard,[19] he was rather proud of his correspondence with Bernard, and was glad of the opportunity to spread abroad the text of the *Apologia*, especially among his fellow canons.[20]

What title did the *Apologia* have in its first and second editions? St Bernard himself describes the work as an *apologia* in Letter eighteen.[21] In the *Vita Prima*, Geoffroy of Auxerre uses the term *Apologeticus*,[22] and in fact it is this title that is used most frequently by the manuscripts, especially the older ones, though *Liber Apologeticus* and *Apologia*, which Bernard himself used, are common enough. There is a whole group of English manuscripts, several of which are quite old, which call the tract the *Epistola de discreta varietate ordinis monastici, et de non iudicando alterius servos, et de superfluitate monachorum* (a letter on the different varieties to be found within the monastic order, on not judging another's servants, and on the excesses of monks). In a few isolated instances the tract is given a generic title, such as *Epistola de vita monastica*.[23]

Most of the manuscripts divide the different sections of the tract by means of headings or *capitula*. One set of these, which comprises ten headings altogether and is attested to by the oldest manuscripts of all regions, has been included in the critical edition of the text and in the present translation.

The overhauling of the first edition was completed toward the end of 1125, about the same time that Peter the Venerable published his defense of the monks of Cluny.[24] The question is, did Bernard have a chance to read this tract before he published his own? The

---

19. *Vie de S. Bernard* (Paris: Lecoffre, 1895), I, p. 190.

20. Details concerning the manuscript tradition of the *Apologia* will be found in the introduction to the critical edition, *S. Bernardi Opera*, III, pp. 67–69.

21. *Letter* 18, 5; PL 182:122; trans. James, no. 19, p. 54.

22. *Vita Prima S. Bernardi*, III, 29; PL 185:320.

23. Cf. *S. Bernardi Opera*, III, pp. 73–74. Also, *Recueil*, II (1966), pp. 123–126.

24. This is Letter 28 in G. Constable's edition, *The Letters of Peter the Venerable*, I (Cambridge, Mass.: Harvard University Press, 1967), pp. 52–101. On the "character" of this letter, cf. *ibid.*, II, pp. 270–274.

possibility is not be be excluded, but if he did, he did not allow it to influence his own presentation in any way, either because he wanted to avoid a personal conflict with the abbot of Cluny, or because the tract arrived too late to make any difference. At any rate, the two major contributions to the debate made their appearance at about the same time.

This was not the end of the trouble. Among the various contributions which appeared, there were two direct replies to St Bernard's charges. The first is the *Riposte* attributed to Hugh of Reading and dated 1127–1128.[25] The other is an anonymous work found in an Oxford manuscript placed immediately after the *Apologia*.[26] This second text, unlike the *Riposte*, is not addressed personally to Bernard, nor does it mention him by name or quote him. The author does not dwell on matters of peripheral importance, like food and drink and clothing; he goes straight to the heart of the question and tries to show that there is a place for a religious order which takes account of ordinary human weakness, and which sets more store by prayer than by austerity. It is more profound and more far-reaching than Hugh of Reading's sparkling reply, but in both cases the concern is the same; to defend the honor of a form of monastic life that is followed by the vast majority of monks.

Form and content

In the *Apologia* Bernard wrote with great artistry, making use of a number of literary devices of which the reader must be aware if he is to interpret the tract correctly and have some insight into the mentality of its author.

The tract is divided into two major sections of about the same length. Its development is modeled on the ancient rhetorical ploy

25. Published by Dom André Wilmart, *op. cit.* Cf. C. H. Talbot, "The Date and Author of the *Riposte*" in *Petrus Venerabilis, 1156–1956*, pp. 72–80, where the authorship and date suggested by Wilmart are confirmed.

26. I have published this under the title "Nouvelle réponse du monachisme ancien aux critiques des cisterciens" in *Receuil*, II, p. 69.

whereby an advocate begins his defense by denigrating his client; it is only when the accused is thoroughly discredited in the sight of all that he begins to rehabilitate him and eventually establish his innocence. These tactics were well known among the ancients, and are found occasionally in later writers, Shakespeare for example.[27] The Black Monks are delighted to hear their Cistercian critics rebuked, but when Bernard swings round to attack the Cluniacs, they find themselves losing favor irretrievably. In his denunciation Bernard makes use of several technical devices, such as the *praeteritio* and the *attestatio rei visae*.[28] One instance of the latter was so powerful that Bernard felt constrained to temper it when he was revising the first edition.[29]

It should be noted that although the *Apologia* looks like a case for the defense, it is really satire. Toward the end of the tract, Bernard shows that he has in mind the correction, not only of the Cluniacs, but also of those of stricter life who had become slanderers. After drawing together the threads of his argument he returns to this point at the end, showing that he is indeed thinking of both parties: "This is what I think about your Order and ours" (No. 31).

From beginning to end, therefore, the *Apologia* is written strictly according to plan. Its structure is indicated not only by the paragraph headings, but also by transitional passages of which the one that marks the break between the two major divisions takes up a whole paragraph (No. 15).

Within the two main sections there is a logical development from

---

27. *The Merchant of Venice*, act 4, scene 1; *Julius Caesar*, act 3, scene 2.

28. A. Forcellini defines *praeteritio* as "a rhetorical device by which we say that we are unwilling to speak of some matter and that we intend to omit reference to it altogether, and then go on to speak of it at length" (*Totius latinitatis lexicon* [London, 1828], II, p. 249). There are examples of *attestatio* in the *Apologia*, nos. 21 and 27. The term *videas*, which begins a clause in no. 21, has many parallels, e.g. Sermon 24 on the Song of Songs, nos. 3 and 4 (*S. Bernardi Opera*, I, p. 153, §8; p. 155, §14; trans. A. Luddy, *St. Bernard's Sermons on the Canticle of Canticles* [Dublin: Browne & Nolan, 1920]). On this, see L. Arbusow, *Colores Rhetorici* (Göttingen, 1948), p. 120, no. 19, "Die 'Cernes'-Formel," with examples of expressions beginning with *videas* and *cernes*.

29. Cf. *infra*, pp. 24f.

generic and doctrinal considerations to concrete practical problems. It may be represented schematically as follows:

A) 1–4   Bernard speaks of his own dispositions and his reasons for writing.

   5   A theological exposition on the theme of unity and plurality in the Church.

  6–9   Application to the various orders of monks.

10–12 The universal necessity of charity.

13–14 A warning to Cistercians not to attach more importance to observances than to the practice of humility and charity.

 15   *Transition.*

B) 16–18 Some general remarks on Cluniac observance.

 19   Comparison with ancient monasticism.

20–23 Food.

24–26 Clothing.

 27   The vain display of their abbots.

28–29 The cost of their buildings.

30–31 *Epilogue.*

Bernard realized that the tract was incomplete, that much more could be added. He takes advantage of its premature conclusion, however, to advance a few thoughts on the need for mutual frankness and charity. He begins on a confident note, but at the end he speaks solemnly of the right of everyone to tell another the truth about himself, and the duty of everyone to accept such admonitions when they come to him. In this way Bernard contrives to convert a mere literary convention into a telling lesson in sincerity.

Historians of art, literature and monasticism are especially interested in the second half, even though the other is richer in doctrine. It is possible that the first part was intended only as a preparation for the denunciations that were to follow, at least in the opinion of a twentieth-century critic. As far as he was concerned, Bernard was writing with all the skill of an orator:

He speaks in a way that might lead simple and superficial readers astray.

What form is it that has the function of concealing the meaning from the reader, or from those who hear it read?

The ancient masters of rhetoric called it "insinuation." It was used in defending a client who was so unpopular with the audience that they did not wish to hear his defense. The advocate of the accused began by taking sides with the opposition. Later on, by a skillful maneuvering of words he switches sides and begins to attack what he had helped to build up, and shows him to be innocent whom he had at first condemned.[30]

The fact is that Bernard's expressions of regard for Cluny, and his denunciation of its enemies served to heighten the effect of his diatribe against its abuses. With such a preparation, the attack strikes home more surely, and when the reader puts down the tract, his impression is determined almost exclusively by the invective. Everything—even Bernard's praise of Cluny, sincere though it was—contributes to make the *Apologia* a real lampoon, and its author's mastery of language assured that it would be a tremendous success.

The literary genre

Two things must be considered to arrive at a just estimate of the worth of the *Apologia*. The first is the literary genre which Bernard adopted for his tract, the second is the perfection of style that he was able to give it.

It was unthinkable for ancient and medieval writers not to base their composition on fixed rules and models appropriate to their purpose. It is these that determine the literary genre.[31]

30. *Dialogus inter Cluniacensem Monachum et Cisterciensem de Diversis utriusque Ordinis Observantiis,* Martène and Durrand, *Thesaurus Novorum Anecdotorum,* V, col. 1577. On *insinuatio,* cf. *Rhethor. ad Herenn.,* I, VI, 9.

31. I have devoted a chapter in *The Love of Learning and the Desire for God* (New York: Fordham University Press, 1961) to the subject of literary genres in monastic authors (ch. 8, pp. 153–188).

Dom André Wilmart, a very able judge of medieval Latin literature, describes the *Apologia* as a *vrai chef-d'oeuvre du genre pamphletaire*.[32] This fearless controversialist, he continues, has produced a work "more like satire than not, for there is scarcely any other word to describe the vigor of such outrageous sarcasm."[33] Did Bernard's contemporaries think the same? The only contender on the Cluniac side to refute the charges of the *Apologia* in detail, as far as we know, was the author of the *Riposte*. He states his case brilliantly and with a great deal of sincerity, and in the opinion of unbiased judges, sustains it successfully. He does not disguise his admiration for Bernard, but he does regret the tone in which he wrote. Twice in the work he describes the *Apologia* as satire.[34] Another monk of the same century gives the function of satire as reprimand: *satira propter reprehensionem*.[35]

Satire or diatribe is a bequest from ancient literary tradition. It is designedly a work in which harsh things are said in order that good may result,[36] a matter in which it is easy to go too far. As Horace himself wrote, "There are some people who say my satire is far too severe, that it goes beyond all reasonable limits. . . ."[37] Even though there is no actual untruth in the satire, exaggeration is almost inevitable; it is part of the game.[38] To condemn its use in the *Apologia* the author of the *Riposte* had only to recall Persius and Juvenal, especially as Bernard had quoted the former, framing his very words.[39] The critic is correct when he says that Bernard is using irony,[40] enjoying himself by writing seriously about things

32. "A real masterpiece of the pamphlet style"—refers to a literary style characterized by its brevity and satire. The pamphlet has been used by many famous authors to put a point across on a subject of current interest. Jonathan Swift is perhaps the best-known to English readers.

33. *Riposte*, pp. 298–299.

34. Ed. Wilmart, *ibid.*, l. 8, p. 309; l. 507, p. 322.

35. *Ibid.*, p. 303, note 2.

36. Estienne defines satire as *carmen maledicum ad carpenda hominum vitia.* Cf. *Thesaurus Linguae Latinae* (Basle, 1743), IV, p. 169.

37. *Satire*, II, i, 1–2.

38. *Riposte*, l. 55–56, p. 318; the word *exaggeratio* occurs in l. 1015, p. 335.

39. *Apologia*, no. 22, quotes Persius, *Satire*, II, 69.

40. *Riposte*, l. 947–949, p. 334.

that are really funny.[41] For example, in his remarkable description of Cluniac egg cookery, Bernard exhibits an extraordinary sense of the comic and doubtlessly won an easy laugh.[42] The copiers entered into his mood and bolstered his formulas in various ways. One of them even added a new item to the list of egg-dishes. Bernard had written: "They might be fried or roasted or stuffed," and the copier added *nunc mollia*, "they might be cooked soft." He was a Norman, and it may be that he had read the *Riposte*, which was most probably written by Hugh of Reading, a French monk in England. The *Riposte* also mentions the matter of soft or hard eggs, *mollia aut dura*,[43] which were the masterpieces of the Cluniac kitchens. The additions in the Fécamp manuscript would therefore be explained by a reminiscence of the text of the *Riposte*.

The picture of gluttons stuffed so full of exotic foods that they cannot take any more is commonplace in satire. In general the authors of the gastronomic poems seem to develop the same themes, the search for bizarre and unusual foods, the cooking until it is "just right," the fine art of sauce-concoction, which is so important because it is a means of transforming the natural taste of the food.[44]

Monastic authors treating of such banquets follow the same general pattern. Long before the *Apologia* Peter Damian penned the following vigorous passage:

> It has displeased me a great deal to see the way monks in many monasteries behave. They are in excellent health, without the slightest need for medical care, yet today they will have a physician let blood, tomorrow they will be using swallows, and then every day will see them with some new remedy. Meanwhile the wheat must be ground fine, and cakes gently cooked for them over ashes. The rivers and the seas must be combed, and there is no let-up for the markets, the ocean's depths are being emptied

41. *Ibid.*, l. 684, p. 327.
42. *Ibid.*, l. 408, p. 320.
43. *Ibid.*, l. 434–437, p. 320.
44. Horace, *Sat.*, II, viii, 28: *longe dissimilem noto celantia sucum*. Cf. *Sat.* II, iv, 38, 40–50, 63–64.

of fish. The fact that the supply of fish has ceased is regarded as an unfortunate mishap, for a heavy demand leads to new sources and new sources lead to greater needs. Meanwhile every living thing on land and sea is brought to slaughter, and it is time to look round for a suitable cook. He must be one who has a knack of controlling the fire so that the heat goes right into the bones while the flesh is not scorched; the heat must penetrate inside, but without harming the outside. What else can be said? Those who sit down to such a meal, or perhaps recline for it, feast until they are so sick to their stomach that they can eat no more. Before they were only pretending, but now they are really sick.[45]

The mild-mannered Peter the Venerable, a contemporary of St Bernard, could not resist writing a page in the same vein:

From all directions they converge, like kites or vultures they quickly make their way to wherever they detect the smoke of a kitchen fire, or their nostrils catch the smell of roasting meat. . . . They are sick of beans and cheese and eggs and even fish, all they want are the flesh-pots of Egypt. The table of holy monks is covered with pork, roasted or boiled, fat heifers, rabbits, hares and the best goose of the gaggle, chicken and every conceivable farmyard bird or beast. After a time even these lose their savor, familiarity breeds contempt. Then they are after foreign delicacies that are fit for a king. Nowadays a monk is satisfied only by venison and the flesh of such wild animals as boars and bears. Hunters must be called in to comb the forests, and fowlers to trap pheasant and partridge and turtledoves, lest the servant of God die of starvation. Take care that none of his whims is left unsatisfied, otherwise he will surely perish. . . . The estates of Cluny are not enough to provide for our lavish banquets, so that it looks as though we shall have to sell off some of the land and its appurtenances to satisfy the monks' appetites. They spend their whole time idling and feasting and preparing themselves for never-ending torments.[46]

Finally we might have a look at a passage from the *Apologia*:

45. *Opusc.* 49, 6; PL 145:726c.
46. *Letter* 161; Constable, *op. cit.*, p. 389.

At table, while the mouth is filled with food, the ears are nourished with gossip so absorbing that all moderation in eating is forgotten. Meanwhile course after course is brought in. Only meat is lacking, and to compensate for this, two huge servings of fish are given. You might have thought that the first was sufficient, but even the recollection of it vanishes, once you have started on the second. . . . Once the palate is attracted to piquant flavors, ordinary things begin to pall; but if there is question of unusual flavors, desire is as quickly aroused as if the meal had not yet begun. The selection of dishes is so exciting that the stomach does not realize that it is being overtaxed. . . . Who could describe all the ways in which eggs are tampered with or tortured, or the care that goes into turning them one way and then turning them back? They might be cooked soft, hard, or scrambled. They might be fried, roasted, and occasionally they are stuffed. Sometimes they are served with other foods, and sometimes on their own. What reason can there be for all this variation except the gratification of a jaded appetite? . . . Three or four times during a meal you might see a cup brought in, half-full, so that the different wines can be sampled, more by aroma than by taste. It is not swallowed, but only caressed, since a seasoned palate can quickly distinguish one wine from another, and select the stronger. It is even alleged to be the custom in some monasteries to give the community honeyed or spiced wine on the major feasts. Is this also on account of stomach troubles? . . . When the monk gets up from table and the swollen veins in his temple begin to throb, all he is fit for is to go back to bed. After all, if you force a man to come to the Office of Vigils before his digestion is complete, all you will extract from him is a groan instead of a tone.[47]

This is the picture of the monastic refectory independently sketched out for us by three reformers of the eleventh and twelfth centuries. Are we therefore obliged to regard their descriptions as historical accounts from which we may garner details of monastic menus for the period and locality in which they wrote? All that can be established from these three invectives is a common regard for

47. *Apologia*, nos. 20–21. With regard to the literal meaning of the texts, it is scarcely necessary to underline the discrepancy between Bernard, who grants that meat was abstained from, and Peter the Venerable, who says that it was not.

austerity, expressed in each case in the same literary form, that of satire. None of these authors could resist the pleasure of writing an effortless page of good prose. The author of the *Riposte* rather grumpily suggests that Bernard put a good deal of effort into his description of Cluniac egg cookery.[48] However, the passage in question is one of the rare parts of the *Apologia* which was left unchanged in the second edition; it was perfect from the start. The literary excellence of the tract is obtained at the expense of justice, since the reproaches are really harsher than they should have been; it is very difficult to ridicule something without going too far. This was why Hugh of Reading criticized the whole second part of the *Apologia;* he thought that Bernard should have put a curb on his talent.[49]

It is very important to know what was going on in Bernard's own mind. Dom Wilmart, who was so harsh in his condemnation of the general tone of the *Apologia*, is very understanding when he comes to examine Bernard's intentions. "St. Bernard," he writes, "was a sort of visionary who instinctively set himself on a plane higher than that of immediate realities, who used to walk past people without even noticing them. In the same way he was able to give offense without being aware of it."[50] The only explanation one can offer is to point to Bernard's own zeal, his love for perfection, and his impatience with mediocrity; he wished that all monks would attain the loftiest heights of austerity. There is a certain amount of unreality in such an aspiration, which means that his criticisms were unfair to some degree. Even this is only the darker side of something that is essentially positive. Hugh of Reading took all the jibes of the *Apologia* rather seriously, but Bernard and William of St Thierry were not fooled by them: they knew them for what they were. The author of the *Riposte* was right to stand up for Cluny's reputation; he also had a high regard for his own Order. He was right on a literary level; if the *Apologia* wishes to paint a picture of monastic behavior, it is false and inaccurate. But on the plane

48. *Riposte*, l. 415–422, p. 320.   49. *Ibid.*, l. 743f., p. 327.
50. *Ibid.*, p. 298, note 4.

of the spiritual, which was Bernard's natural habitat, the *Apologia* rings true. The literary skill which Bernard lavished on the tract is only a means of expressing an ideal, for which monks of all ages should be grateful. In fact it was the Black Monks, the object of his attack, who were most instrumental in spreading his writings,[51] so well aware were they of the extraordinary combination of holiness and literary talent which these works embody.

The exaggerations to be found in the *Apologia* were no more than one would expect to find in a satire; both Bernard and his readers understood this. Dom Mège, a solemn Maurist of the seventeenth century, felt obliged to counter Bernard's description of the different ways of cooking eggs, with the observation that St Benedict had allowed two cooked dishes at each meal, "so that those who cannot eat one can make their meal on the other."[52] This is hardly necessary. It is better to let the matter pass with a smile, and concentrate on catching Bernard's lesson on simplicity and austerity. The indignation proper to the satirical author likewise explains his impassioned tone. The descriptions of the Cluniac at table or his abbot on a trip are not meant to be more factual than the twelve proud men who people the second part of *The Steps of Humility*. E. Faral's remark on this matter is excellent:

The rhetoric of the ancients included description among the means by which an orator was able to persuade or move his audience. This view was widely held in the Middle Ages. When an author produced a descriptive passage, his aim was to act on the sensibilities and the imagination of his reader. Virtually none of the medieval authors, in Latin or vernacular, described things for the mere pleasure of definition or demonstration or to convey an objective picture of things. This is why people go astray when they try to find in them a faithful and meaningful portrayal of things and events that exist no longer. The fact is that neither historians not archeologists will find them particularly

51. I have given some details on the role played by Benedictines in the circulation of St Bernard's writings in *Receuil*, II, pp. 19–34, 141–148.

52. *Rule*, ch. 39, 4. Dom Mège, *Commentaire sur la Règle de S. Benoît* (Paris, 1687), p. 534.

instructive, since their whole concern was to stir up emotional reactions in the souls of their readers.[53]

Within the limits of the literary genre he had adopted, the themes Bernard developed were monastic. For example, his protests against sculpture and other images inside the monastery were part of a long monastic tradition going back to Cassian.[54] His indignation at the immensity of some of the buildings he encountered can be paralleled in the writings of reformers of every age,[55] and also in hagiography.[56] His allusion to Cluniac wine-sampling has many precedents.[57] Consider Bernard's description of the church at Cluny: "I shall say nothing about the soaring heights, and extravagant lengths and unnecessary widths of the churches, nothing about their expensive decorations and their novel images. . . ."[58] Here we see Bernard making use of three rhetorical devices. The first

53. E. Faral, "Sidoine Apollinaire et la technique littéraire du moyen âge" in *Miscellanea Giovanni Mercati* (Vatican City: Polyglot Press, 1946), vol. II, p. 568.

54. Cassian, *Conferences*, X, 5; C.S.E.L. 13, pp. 10–16; trans. C. S. Gibson in *Nicene and Post-Nicene Fathers*, second series, vol. XI, p. 403. On Cassian and others as sources of St Bernard's use of *acedia*, see S. Wenzel, "Acedia in 1100–1200" in *Traditio*, 22 (1966), pp. 86–89.

55. I have given the texts in *Aux sources de la spiritualité occidentale*, pp. 180–184.

56. In his *Life* of Eigil of Fulda, Candidus of Fulda puts into the mouth of Emperor Louis the Pious a discourse in which, citing St John Chrysostom, he advises monks henceforward to give their money to the poor instead of constructing *immensa aedificia* (ed. J. Mabillon in *Acta Sanctorum O.S.B.*, vol. IV [Venice, 1735], i, p. 223, note 11). See also *Monumenta Germaniae Historiae*, *SS.*, XV, 226–227. On this latter text, see J. Semmler in *Corpus consuetudinum monasticarum* (Sieburg, 1964), vol. I, p. 230. In William of Malmesbury's *Life of St Wulstan*, the development of the theme is summarized by Mabillon in a marginal note: *Modestus in aedificiis, etiam sacris; op. cit.*, VI, ii, pp. 835f.

57. *Apologia*, no. 21. The first edition had read: *vina dum potando ac probando potantur*. Hugeburge's *Life of St Wunibald* has: *Parvum vini potum utere solebat, ut iam pene non bibendo, sed probando, maiores patiebat gustando continentiam quam aliter non recipiendo* (*Monumenta Germaniae Historiae*, *SS.*, VI, iii, 7–8). The expression that Hugeburge of Heidenheim uses to connote abstemiousness, Bernard uses to indicate excess. Cf. Geoffrey of Vinsauf's expression *nec vina probans*, in *Poetrio nova* (c. 1793), quoted by Faral, *op. cit.*, p. 574.

58. *Apologia*, no. 28. Other examples of such accumulation of epithets are found in Faral, *op. cit.*, pp. 574ff.

is the *praeteritio*, which involves affirming one's reluctance to speak about the matter at issue.[59] The second is the accumulation of epithets, *immensas altitudines, immoderatas longitudines, supervacuas latitudines, sumptuosas depolitiones, curiosas depolitiones.* Finally, there is his use of assonance, well controlled since he realizes that too much of it can become tiresome. In the passage which speaks of "the mingling of harmony and discord" in the Church, there is a distinct possibility that Bernard is repeating a formula of Ovid.[60] Bernard illustrates the theme of diversity in unity by recourse to Jn 14:2, "In my Father's house there are many rooms." An examination of St Augustine's commentary on this verse reveals that Bernard has certainly been inspired by it when writing the *Apologia*.[61] There are the same ideas, several parallel formulas, and the same reference to 1 Cor 15:41, "Star differs from star in glory." To gauge the familiar liberty the abbot of Clairvaux allowed himself in the use of his source, one only has to compare the *Apologia* with the tract *De diversis ordinibus Ecclesiae*.[62] The author develops the same theme and uses the same sources, but he lacks wealth of biblical imagery that Bernard has added to Augustine, and which makes the *Apologia* at once more striking and more lyrical.

The style of the Apologia

One thing we do know for certain about the *Apologia* is that Bernard took great pains in its composition. He submitted it to the

59. See note 28.
60. *Metamorph.*, I, 432–433.
　Cumque sit ignis aquae pugnax, vapor umidus omnes
　　Recreat et discors concordia *fetibus apta est.*
Bernard's text read: *intelligens denique Ecclesia hanc suam quodammodo discordem concordiam concerdemve discordiam.*
　61. St Augustine, *In Joannem,* 67, 2–3; *Corp. Christ.,* no. 36, pp. 495f.; trans. J. Gibb and J. Innes in *Nicene and Post-Nicene Fathers,* first series, vol. VII, pp. 321f.
　62. *De diversis ordinibus Ecclesiae,* I; PL 213:813. The author seems to have been Rimbaud, a canon regular of Liège, writing between 1125 and 1130. This is C. Dereine's opinion: "Les origines de Prémontré" in *Rev. d'hist. ecclés.,* 42 (1947), pp. 359–360, 376–377.

C

examination of his two friends, and then re-worked it before bringing it to completion. Since we have the original text which was
privately circulated and the edition that Bernard eventually
published, we are able to compare the two and discover what
Bernard had in mind when he made the alterations.

From the start the *Apologia* was written with great verve. The
revision of the text only increased its vigor. Sixty-four corrections
were involved altogether, not counting insufficiently attested
variants that can be traced to copiers' errors. Nearly every page has
one or two changes, at an average frequency of one every ten lines.
What is the point in such changes? Often it is hard to tell. Why,
for example, did Bernard replace *si quid me scriptitare iussistis* and
non ut *negligerem* by *si qua me scriptitare iussistis* and *non* quia *negligerem?* The author made these subtle changes when rereading the
text months later, and it is not always possible for us to work out
why. We are not aware of any improvement in grammar, content
or rhythm, since we are not able to read the text with the accent,
intonation and pronunciation that his contemporaries used, much
less with his own. Bernard's intentions in making these revisions
remain his own secret. Most of the corrections are small. The word
order is changed nine times, either to improve the sound of it, or
to bring out a nuance or heighten a contrast between two words.

It is fairly easy to go through the critical edition of the *Apologia*
and draw up a list of all the corrections and then classify them as
grammatical, rhythmic, or stylistic. Such facts are a means of
studying Bernard's methods of composition. For the moment it is
sufficient to say that the changes rarely modify the meaning of the
passage concerned. In one place the abbot of Clairvaux eliminates
a phrase which had underlined the fact that he had been an eye-
witness to the abuses he was describing. He replaced, "It is embarrassing to speak of such things that, had I not seen them with
my own eyes, I would scarcely have credited," with "It is embarrassing to speak of these things, but it should be more embarrassing
still to do them. If you are ashamed to hear them mentioned, you
needn't be too ashamed to amend." The second expression is even
more severe than the first, but its substitution at least forestalled

the criticism that Bernard was ungrateful for the hospitality he had received at Cluny. Most of the other minor corrections tell us less about what was going on in Bernard's mind than about his exactitude in the choice of language. This trait is often underestimated, but it is really very revealing.

Apart from the less important changes, Bernard introduced two new passages in his second edition. The second of these is simply inserted in the text without requiring any modifications. The other passage required a few slight changes in the paragraph that followed it. Here, as in Sermons twenty-four and seventy-one on the *Song of Songs*, in the prologues to the *Sermons on Psalm ninety*, and the *Sermons in Praise of the Virgin Mary*, the seam is imperceptible. Bernard was, as he admitted, a master of "invisible mending" (*resarcire*).

Both the additions are in the second part. There is no tempering of his invective. In the first Bernard denounces with a series of scriptural texts the illusion that allowed laxity to pass itself off as discretion. The second introduces some new material which Bernard had not foreseen when drawing up the original plan. Apparently he had picked up some details which he had not known before. It was reported to him that there were hale and hearty young monks who had transferred to the infirmary for the sole purpose of qualifying for the mitigations allowed the sick, notwithstanding the fact that the Cluniac regime was never particularly severe. To earn their places at the better laden tables these monks had to support a pretense of illness with the aid of walking sticks, so that it might look as though they were exhausted. "Should we laugh or cry at such foolishness?"

Finally, when reading any of St Bernard's writings we must take note of the individual nature of each. His own contemporaries were able to do this more readily than we, since we have lost contact with classical literary tradition. The *Apologia* is not a factual document meant to convey details of the actual state of Cluniac observance. It is a caricature, designed to correct them. There is a certain amount of sarcasm and exaggeration, and it is always possible that these be carried too far—though this is not the case in the present instance—but even so, it is a legitimate method of composition, and we must not allow ourselves to be led astray by it. Bernard is only one of many who have developed the theme of the fantastic feast, though he does it rather well, and in his own particular style. He has no intention of giving an objective analysis of the Cluniac diet; he merely gives an amusing lesson in the demands of monastic austerity. In the various monasteries where this tract was found, it is probably true to say that the monks were grateful to St Bernard for making his spirituality so entertaining.

The contemporary relevance of the Apologia

We have already discussed St Bernard's teaching in the *Apologia*, and the classical, biblical, patristic, and monastic sources he followed. With Bernard there is no separation of content from literary expression; he is at one and the same time a theologian and an artist, and style was as much part of his writing as the truth he expounded.

All that remains to be done is to indicate briefly the dominant themes of the *Apologia*, the key ideas which allow us to catch hold of its message. These have to do with Christ, monasticism as a way of Christian life, the role of monasticism in the life of the Church, and the way monastic life should be lived.

As usual Bernard's approach is Christocentric. He speaks of seeking only Christ, hoping in him alone (No. 1), of carrying his cross, sharing in his suffering, and imitating his humility (No. 2), poverty (No. 3), and obedience (No. 6), so as to share his joy in the present life and his glory in the next. Bernard insists very strongly throughout the *Apologia* on poverty and he treats of it at length toward the end (No. 28). This alone is sufficient to give the tract some importance for Christians of today. Poverty is understood in its deeper meaning, as it is embodied in Christ, who is its origin and model.[63] Over and above the rejection of superfluities, this

63. I have given various biblical and patristic texts on this point in *Aspects of Monasticism, Yesterday and Today* (Cistercian Studies Series 7), ch.3.

virtue involves the renunciation of all personal privilege, self-complacence, superiority, pride and self-satisfaction. In the *Apologia* Bernard recalls the teaching of Jesus on simplicity of heart as opposed to hypocrisy, pharisaism, and judgment of others which is not based on concern for their welfare (Nos. 10–11); on inwardness (No. 12), as well as the superiority of heartfelt love and purity of intention over all outward observance (Nos. 13–14).

Such love, which is God, comes from the Father, is made manifest in the Son, and was communicated by the Holy Spirit to the monks of old, the Fathers of monastic life. It was from them that monasticism began; they invented it, they were its begetters. It might be said that they were the channels by which the Holy Spirit was communicated to their followers. A monk has only to look back to their charisms, their experience, their example, their teaching, to the ideal that has always found expression in the Church. This is why Bernard insists on a fidelity to the holy founders—either those of primitive monasticism or those of more recent times (Nos. 4, 19, 23). This too is very much to the point in these days when Vatican II has asked all religious to do precisely what Bernard recommends.

At the same time, Bernard does not set any one of them up as an absolute model. It is collectively that their example has validity. Their common ideal finds different expressions which are all legitimate insofar as they are both effects and signs of the mystery of the one Church of Jesus Christ. Today there is much talk about pluralism. The idea is not new, and it has never been formulated so powerfully and at such length and with such artistry as in the passage of the *Apologia* where Bernard justifies—or rather admires and praises—the diversity of observances to be found within a single ideal. The love of Christ always present in the Church is the life of the Church; it never ceases to promote the growth of the Church and to raise up new forms of life in the Holy Spirit. This continual growth is the means by which the Church maintains its steady progress toward full maturity. It is an eschatological anticipation of the life of the heavenly city that Bernard portrays, drawing on the Book of Revelation, St Paul, and the Prophets. This vision of the Church, charged as it is with biblical poetry, draws from Bernard pages which are as beautiful as any he wrote, and which are among the most beautiful in the entire literature of ecclesiology.

The practical teaching on monastic life in the second part is nothing more than the embodiment of the theological principles already enunciated. Two of the paragraph headings (Nos. 16, 24) show that his attack is directed against superfluities, against whatever is not required by monastic life as such—as related to the hope one has in Christ, and to one's love for him, which enables a man to give up whatever does not contribute to the realization of this ideal, and even more so whatever impedes it. Hence discretion is to be understood not as a mitigation which paves the way to an easy life, but a new decision regarding what is consistent with the ideal, and what is not. Such a decision will vary according to time, place, and culture. The concrete establishing of what is superfluous and what is not, will change, but the principle behind such a decision is the same. Bernard applies this principle to conditions of his own age, to food and clothing, and to the style appropriate to abbots when abroad, and who would deny that the last point, at least, is perennial?

There is one point to which historians attach special importance, although it is only secondary in relation to the principles involved, and this is Bernard's attitude toward Church art and architecture. It is here perhaps that the exaggeration proper to satire looms largest. Bernard's general notion is that as far as monks are concerned, beauty should be simple and unaffected, and as pure as the God it reflects. Here we must beware of making over-facile generalizations about Benedictine "sumptuousness" and Cistercian "austerity." The fact is that most monastic churches are modest enough, both in size and design. In particular, the Cluniac dependencies were unassuming, built according to the current style. By way of exception, there were a few basilicas which were centers of pilgrimage, like Cluny and Saint-Benoît-sur-Loire. In these their size was increased to cater to the non-monastic purpose they fulfilled, and their decor was often similar to that of cathedrals and parish churches. The Cistercians wanted all their abbeys built in out-of-the-way places, and they did not allow visitors access to their churches. This is why simplicity remained supreme.[64] However, as communities grew, the Cistercians too were obliged to erect vast monasteries which were sometimes larger and just as expensive as those built by other orders. The solid and impressive, but tremendously harmonious proportions of Fontenay, which was built according to Bernard's intentions, is one of the best examples of the style of architecture he was calling for. One curious fact is, however, that among the twelfth-century monasteries remaining today, the most modest and most in line with Bernard's ideas are not those founded from Clairvaux, but places like Senanque and Le Thoronet, which derive from Cîteaux.

Finally, to bring the *Apologia* to a close Bernard writes briefly on a subject which he will be treating in his tract, *Monastic Obligations and Abbatical Authority*, and in many of his letters; the transfer of monks from one order to another. The few remarks he makes here have to be judged in the light of his more detailed teaching, as well as his own practice in this matter.

* * *

Like every great work that bears the impress of genius and sanctity, the *Apologia* never grows old. It is as young and fresh and relevant today as when it was first published. To appreciate this, however, it is necessary to appreciate the double aspect of Bernard's greatness; on the one hand, his literary genius which enabled him to handle satire, humor and sarcasm with much mastery, on the other the purity of his experience of the mystery of Christ in the Church which gave him a basis for distinguishing the essential from what was peripheral. The only thing that cannot be replaced is love, everything else can and does change. If today monks could help each other in this task of discerning what is central and what is not— and this is what *aggiornamento* is all about—they would be rendering each other a service that would bear witness to their common

64. Further details on this point can be found in J. Hubert et al., *Moissac et l'occident au XI*e *siècle* (Toulouse, 1964), pp. 47–58.

seeking after God in humility. In this way the frankness that Bernard asks for in the last lines of the *Apologia* would be continually realized in the Church. "Whatever is praiseworthy in your monks I praise and extol. On the other hand, to you and to my other friends I point out whatever is worthy of reproach, in order that it may be corrected. This is not slander, but candor, and I ask you very earnestly, always to do the same for us."

Jean Leclercq OSB

Clervaux Abbey,
Luxembourg

TRANSLATOR'S NOTE

Something should be said about the principles underlying the present translation. I shall merely indicate the broad lines of policy, leaving to the reader the task of assessing the extent of its application, and the validity of its premises.

It is impossible to produce an English version of the *Apologia* without a compromise of some sort. So happily married is the content of the *Apologia* to the genius of the Latin language, that a very literal translation is most undesirable. Replacing the sparkling verve of the original with a limp and prolix English rendering, would destroy the *Apologia's* eminent readability. To a large extent also, it would undermine the plausibility of Bernard's position. The *Apologia* is not primarily a logical presentation of certain basic monastic values; it is more like an appeal to the heart for their implementation. It is meant to evoke a reaction and a response in the reader. A translation fails if it reproduces the logical content in hollow isolation, incorporating nothing of the spirit or zest of the original.

In practice the best results are achieved by keeping the prose moving, by keeping it bright and brisk, and not too ponderous. This may involve the modification of sentence structure or a redistribution of elements within a period. In some cases it was desirable to replace a string of rhetorical questions with emphatic statements. Words and phrases which serve the sole function of lubricating the Latinity have been suppressed where they would impede the flow of English. It was with more regret that I allowed some precious nuances to slip away. In particular, many biblical reminiscences had to be relinquished. These scriptural undertones are so characteristic of St Bernard that it was unfortunate to lose them. In the Latin they were valuable aids in holding the reader's attention, as it were punctuating a passage with pleasant spasms of recognition. But there is no common English text today that can serve in this way. The same holds for the puns and ploys which Bernard habitually scatters through his prose. These agreeable by-products of his style must be subordinated to the primary purpose of his writing; in translation this usually means their suppression. It is unfortunate, but unavoidable.

In the notes I have tried to give something of the *Apologia's* wider context, and to clear up any misunderstandings that are liable to occur. Contrasting positions adopted by other personalities in the controversy are indicated briefly, as well as parallel passages in Bernard's other writings. The principal scriptural allusions are identified, though it must be recalled that Bernard was using the Vulgate text, which often differs substantially from our modern versions. Direct citations are translated to fit the context, though where there are alternative systems of reference (e.g. in the Psalms), I have followed the Revised Standard Version.

The translation itself is based on the critical Latin edition published by Jean Leclercq and Henri Rochais in the third volume of the *Sancti Bernardi Opera*.[1] References to other works of St Bernard are, wherever possible, to the critical edition published in this series. Otherwise they are to Mabillon's edition in Migne.[2] As far as I know this is the first complete English translation of the *Apologia;* although, it is true, Ailbe Luddy did include most of it in his *Life*

1. Rome: Editiones Cistercienses, 1963.
2. References to Bernard's works in Migne all occur in vol. 182, so I have simply cited them by column. The same holds for the writings of Peter the Venerable, which are all contained in vol. 189.

and Teaching of St Bernard.[3] For the convenience of English-speaking readers I have also referred to the best available translations of Bernard's other works.[4]

Michael Casey ocso

Tarrawarra Abbey
  Australia

3. Pp. 98–104.

4. Most of Bernard's sermons have been translated by Ailbe Luddy; *St Bernard's Sermons on the Canticle of Canticles,* 2 vols. (Dublin: Browne & Nolan, 1920). *St Bernard's Sermons for the Seasons and the Principal Festivals of the Year,* 3 vols. (Dublin: Browne & Nolan, 1921–1925). For the *De gradibus humilitatis et superbiae,* I have used the version by Geoffrey Webb and Adrian Walker, *The Steps of Humility* (London: Mowbrays, 1956). For the *Letters,* the excellent rendition by Bruno Scott James was the obvious choice; *The Letters of St Bernard of Clairvaux* (London: Burns & Oates, 1952).

AN APOLOGIA TO ABBOT WILLIAM

To the Reverend Father William,[1]
From Brother Bernard, the unworthy servant of the brothers at
Clairvaux,
Greetings in the Lord.

PRIOR TO THIS, if you had asked me to do some writing,
I would not have agreed, or if I had agreed, it would have
been reluctantly. It is not that I care nothing for your requests,
it is simply that I would never have dared to attempt something so
beyond my capabilities. Now that the situation has become really
serious, my former diffidence has vanished. Spurred on by the need
for action, mine is the painful position of having no alternative but
to comply, without worrying about how well I can do it.

How can I possibly keep quiet when I hear your complaints

---

1. William of St Thierry, at whose request the *Apologia* was written, was a
close friend of St Bernard for thirty years, and the first to write his biography.
He was born at Liège about 1085. After studying at Laon for some time, he
entered the Benedictine Abbey of St Nicasius at Rheims. About 1120, he was
elected abbot of St Thierry. In 1135 he entered the Cistercian abbey of Signy,
and died there in 1148. He was the author of several works, the most famous
of which is the "Golden Epistle" to the Carthusians of Mont-Dieu. Cf.
Jean-Marie Déchanet, *William of Saint-Thierry, The Man and His Work*,
Cistercian Studies Series 10. Louis Bouyer, *The Cistercian Heritage* (London:
Mowbrays, 1958), pp. 67–124.

against us? You say that we poor men who are clothed in rags[2] dare, from our holes in the ground, as Jerome says,[3] to pass judgment on the world. You say that we insult your glorious Order,[4] and shamelessly slander the holy men who belong to it and are more deserving of our praise. You say that from our base obscurity[5] we dare to scoff at the world's luminaries. This is more unbearable still. If it is true, then under sheep's disguise we are, not ravenous wolves, but nibbling fleas and gnawing moths. We are afraid to make a public outcry, yet, with our whispered calumny we secretly eat away good men's reputations.

If this is how things stand, what will it profit us to be put to death without cause all the day long, and accounted as sheep for the slaughter?[6] If, I repeat, we are proud pharisees who look down on others, and even despise men better than ourselves, we can expect no advantage from a diet that is lean and unlovely, nor from the well-known cheapness and roughness of our clothes. The sweat of daily toil, our continual fasts and vigils, and all the austerity of our way of life will do us no good, unless it happen that we are per-

---

2. *In pannis et semicinctiis.* The first Cistercians were famous for their poor clothing. "They rejected what was contrary to the Rule, namely, wide *cucullae,* furs, linen shirts, cowls, breeches. . . ." (*Exordium Parvum,* XV; PL 166: 1507; trans. R. Larkin in Lekai, *The White Monks* [Okauchee: Cistercian Fathers, 1953], p. 262). Cf. *Exordium Magnum,* dist. I, cap. 20; [ed. Griesser (Rome: Editiones Cistercienses, 1961), p. 75, l. 25f.]. The *semicinctium* was probably some sort of loin-cloth worn underneath the robe.

3. Lit. "as *he* says." See introduction, p. 7. The reference is to Jerome's *Letter* 17, 2, C.S.E.L. 64, p. 71; trans. in *Nicene and Post-Nicene Fathers* (Grand Rapids: Eerdmans, 1957, second series, vol. VI, p. 21). Cf. Bernard's *Letter* 48, 3; PL 156c; trans. James, no. 51, p. 81).

4. St Thierry was not, in fact, affiliated to Cluny, even though Bernard speaks in no. 23 of the Fathers of Cluny as "your founders and teachers." The *Apologia* is nominally addressed to all Black Monks, though it is clear that very often Bernard is really thinking of Cluny.

5. *Umbra ignobilitatis;* Bernard often employs the term *umbra* to designate the hidden and obscure character of Cistercian monasticism. For an analysis of the theme, together with relevant bibliographical information, see Jean Leclercq, "La vie cachée" in *Chances de la spiritualité occidentale* (Paris: Cerf, 1966), pp. 279f.

6. Cf. Ps 44:22; "without cause" may derive from Ps 73:13.

forming these works with a view to being seen by men. But Christ says: "I tell you in all truth, these men have already received their reward."[7] For it is certainly true that "if we have hope in Christ in this life alone, we are the most pitiable of all men."[8] Such indeed we are, if by our service of Christ we are seeking glory only in the present life.

2. Poor remnant of a man that I am! I try so hard not to be like, or rather not to seem like the rest of men,[9] yet I will receive little for my efforts. In fact, I shall be judged more severely than anybody else. Why hasn't someone discovered a more comfortable way to hell? If we must go there, why shouldn't we join the throng which takes the broad path that leads to death? Then, at least, we could have joy instead of sorrow, before passing into that final sorrow. Oh, how much luckier are they who have no thought for death! They remain steadfast throughout their troubles. They are not upset and afflicted as other men are.[10] Even though sinners will have to suffer forever because of life's joys, at least they enjoyed plenty of the good things of this world. Oh, unhappy are they who carry a cross, not like the Savior, who carried his own, but like the Cyrenian who carried another's.[11] Unhappy the harpers who play, not on their own harps, as do the men in Revelation, but on someone else's, like

---

7. Mt 6:5.   8. 1 Cor 15:19.
9. Cf. Mt 7:13.   10. Cf. Ps 73:4f.
11. The same unfavorable interpretation of Simon's cross-bearing is found in St Bernard's sermon for the feast of St Benedict, no. 6. "Trees that bear fruit which is not their own are hypocrites; like Simon of Cyrene, they carry someone else's cross. This they do under pressure and with no religious intent since they are forced to do unpleasant things by their desire for vain-glory" (*S. Bern. Op.*, V, p. 55; trans. Luddy, *Principal Festivals*, III, pp. 122f.). The theme is treated more amply in one of the passages edited by Dom Séjourné in "Les inédits bernardins du Ms. d'Anchin" (*S. Bernard et son temps*, II [Dijon: Académie des Sciences, Artes, et Belles-Lettres, 1929], p. 270, App. A): "The fourth type of cross is the one which Simon (i.e. the obedient man) carried. He bears all the difficulties of obedience with alacrity, and carries any cross in the same way that he carried the Lord's. He runs and he works because he is under pressure from two implacable task-masters, pride and vain-glory. In the end he will not enjoy the fruit of obedience, since he will not be judged on the basis of his external obedience, but according to his internal obedience and right intention."

hypocrites.[12] Twice unhappy are they who are both proud and poor. Twice unhappy, I repeat, are those who carry Christ's cross without following after him, who share in his sufferings with no thought of imitating his humility.

3. Such people are doomed to a double measure of punishment. In the present life they punish themselves to win the world's praise; in the next, their inward pride will cause them to be thrown into unending torment. They toil with Christ, yet they will not reign with him. Though they imitate Christ in his poverty, they will not share his glory. In their journeying they drink from the stream, but they will never lift up their head in the homeland.[13] They mourn here, but hereafter they will not be comforted.[14] And rightly so. It is not for pride to deck itself out in the swaddling clothes of Jesus' humility.[15] It is true that contact with his childhood is the only remedy for human sinfulness. But what are we to think when pride squeezes itself into the Lord's crib in order to deceive, when instead of innocent whimpers, we find there the evil whispers of slander. The proud men in the Psalm,[16] whose bodies seethe with malice and who are openly adorned with ungodliness and vice are in a better position than we, who try to conceal vice under a cloak of virtue. The man who adds falsehood to his other vices by pretending to be holy, is twice as blameworthy as one who acknowledges his own defects.

Now what shall I say? I am afraid that I myself may be thought guilty on this score, not by you Father, of course, not by you. I know that you understand me as well as any man can in this land of darkness, and in this matter especially, I know that you are aware of what I think. These things that you have often heard orally from me I am committing to writing for the sake of those who do not know me as well as you do, and with whom I have not discussed

---

12. Cf. Rev 14:2.   13. Cf. Ps 110:7.   14. Cf. Mt 5:4.
15. The same metaphor occurs in *Letter* 51: "But now they are looking for simony under the swaddling clothes of the child Jesus" (PL 159a; trans. James, No. 54, p. 83).
16. Ps 73:7.

matters as I have with you. I cannot go round and explain my position to each one individually. Instead, I write this, so that you will have something from me with which to convince them on my behalf of what you yourself know quite definitely from my own lips. There is nothing in my private conversations with you on this subject, that I am afraid to lay before the eyes of all.

II.   4. No one had ever heard me denouncing this Order or murmuring against it. I am always delighted to see any of its members. I receive them with all due honor; I converse with them respectfully, and encourage them in all humility. What I say now is what I have always said. This way of life is holy and good. Chastity is its adornment, discretion its renown. Organized by the Fathers and predestined by the Holy Spirit, it is eminently suited for the saving of souls. How could I possibly condemn or contemn an Order I praise so highly? I remember how, on occasion, I was welcomed as a guest in some monasteries of the Order. I pray that the Lord will reward his servants for the abundant kindness they lavished on me when I was ill, and for the honor they rendered me, which they themselves were more worthy than I to receive. I have asked them to pray for me.[17] I have attended their community meetings.[18] I have spoken a great deal with many of them about the Bible and the salvation of souls, both publicly in chapter, and privately.[19] I have never secretly or openly encouraged anyone to leave that Order and come to ours; in fact, I rebuffed many monks who wanted to come, and if any came knocking, I turned them

17. Apart from oral requests, Bernard ends two of his letters to Peter the Venerable by soliciting the prayers of "the holy brethren of Cluny" (*Letter* 228, 2; PL 398a; trans. James, no. 305, p. 376 and *Letter* 387; PL 591d; trans. James, no. 308, p. 379).

18. Community meetings, *collationes*, are described in J. Leclercq, *The Love of Learning and the Desire for God* (New York: Mentor, 1962), p. 169.

19. Lit. "privately, *in cameris*". The room labeled *camera* in Dr Conant's plan of Cluny (plate IV, in *Petrus Venerabilis, 1156-1956*) measures approx. 100′ × 30′. *Camera* is a generic term covering any sort of room; Bernard is probably referring to small rooms suitable for private consultation.

away.[20] Br Nicholas I sent back to the Abbey of St Nicholas,[21] and you will recall that I returned two of your own monks. Moreover, you know well enough that there were two abbots of the Order who wanted to change, and were even making plans to do so, and that it was only my advice to the contrary that deterred them from resigning. I won't mention any names since you know who they are, and that they are my own close friends.[22] Why should people think or say that I reject an order, when I advise my friends to remain in it, when I send back its monks if they come to us; and from it earnestly ask prayers for myself and accept them with gratitude?

III.   5. Perhaps the mere fact of my belonging to another order is sufficient to give rise to suspicions on this score. But if this is so, it must also be true that you are insulting us by not adopting our way of life. By the same token, we would have to take it for granted that celibates and married folk are at variance, simply because their lives are moderated by different Church laws, and that monks and regulars are always at odds due to differences in observances. We would never guess that Noah, Daniel, and Job share the same kingdom, since we know they followed very different paths of virtue.[23] Finally, we would have to affirm that either Mary or

20. Bernard's practice may be culled from several of his letters, e.g. nos 3, 32ff., 65ff., 253, 382, 396 (trans. James, nos. 3, 33f., 68ff., 328, 419, 428.) Cf. note 172.

21. The abbey of Saint Nicholas-aux-Bois, ruled at this time by Simon, said to be a brother of William of St Thierry, was situated in the diocese of Laon. Br Nicholas may be the monk to whom Bernard refers in one of his letters to Simon (*Letter* 84; PL 205f.; trans. James, no. 86, p. 124).

22. One of these abbots very probably was William himself. His attraction to the Cistercian life dated from his first meeting with Bernard in 1118 (Cf. *Vita Prima* II, cap. vii, no. 33; PL 185:246d). His application to join, made shortly before the composition of the *Apologia*, was rejected by Bernard. Cf. *Letter* 86, 2 (PL 210d; trans. James, no. 88, p. 128).

23. Basing himself on an interpretation of Ezek 14:14 f., Gregory the Great saw in Noah, Daniel and Job types of the different orders in the Church. Noah represented the church authorities, Daniel the religious, and Job the good lay-folk (*Moralia*, I, 20; *Sources chrétiennes*, 32 [Paris, 1952],p. 152). Bernard often employs the same categories: e.g. Sermon 35, *De diversis*

Martha or both failed to please the Lord, since their efforts to do this were so very unlike.[24]

If all this were correct, there would be neither peace nor harmony in the Church, arrayed as it is, like the queen in the Psalm,[25] with a wide variety of religious orders. If it is true that by entering one order, a man is bound to hold the other orders in contempt, or to believe that this is their attitude toward him, how can he possibly find peace and security in his vocation, since it is quite impossible for one man to join all the orders? At the same time, no one order is suitable for everybody.

I am not so dull that I cannot recognize Joseph's robe here. I don't mean the Joseph who freed Egypt from bodily famine, but the one who saved the world from death of soul and body. This robe was famous for its many colors; it was marked out by a glorious variety. The robe was dipped in blood, not goat's blood signifying sin, but lamb's blood, which typifies innocence. This means that it was his own blood, not someone else's. For he, surely, is the meek lamb that was speechless, not before shearers, but before slayers. He

---

(*S. Bernardi Opera*, VI, p. 200); *In Nativ.*, I, 7 (*ibid.*, IV, p. 249); *In Dom. Palm.*, I, 4 (*ibid.*, V, p. 45). The author of the *Nouvelle réponse* proposes a slightly different interpretation of the same three figures (ed. J. Leclercq, *Recueil d'études sur saint Bernard et ses écrits* [Rome: Edizioni di Storia e Letteratura, 1966], II, p. 83). Cf. G. Penco, "Temi ed aspetti ecclesiologici della tradizione monastica" in *Studia Monastica*, 10 (1968), p. 66; P. Deseille, "Théologie de la vie monastique selon S. Bernard" in *Théologie de la vie monastique* (Paris: Aubier, 1961), pp. 519–521.

24. Martha and Mary are the traditional types of the active and the contemplative way of life. For the first phases of the history of the theme, up to the time of Augustine, cf. Daniel Csanyí, "Optima Pars: die Auslegungsgeschichte von Lk 10, 36–42 bei den Kirchenvätern der ersten vier Jahrhunderte" in *Studia Monastica*, 2 (1960), pp. 5–78. Peter the Venerable considers the hard-working Cistercians to have chosen Martha's part (*Letters* I, 28; PL 129a). The author of the *Nouvelle réponse* follows him in this, as in other matters, l. 171f., *op. cit.*, p. 79. The same retort is put in the mouth of the Cluniac in the *Dialogus inter Cluniacensem Monachum et Cisterciensem de Diversis utriusque Ordinis Observantiis* (ed. Martène and Durand, *Thesaurus Novorum Anecdotorum*, V, col. 1569ff.). Cf. Knowles, *Cistercians and Cluniacs*, p. 32. Bernard himself refers to the idea in no. 12.

25. Cf. Ps 45:14.

D

committed no sin, and yet he took away the sins of the world. The text continues: "They sent to Jacob and said, 'We found this. See whether or not it is your son's robe.' "[26] You also Lord, see whether this is your beloved Son's robe. All-powerful Father, recognize the many-colored garment you have made for your Anointed. Some men you have set aside as apostles, others as prophets. Some are preachers of the Gospel, others are pastors or teachers or fulfill some other role in the wondrous decoration of this garment. All contribute to the perfection of the saints, and together all press on toward mature manhood, according to the measure of the age of Christ's fullness.[27] O God, take note also of the dark hue of his precious blood, sprinkled over the garment, the splendid and victorious sign of obedience. "Why," the text asks, "is your apparel all red?" He answers, "Because I have trodden the wine-press alone. From the peoples not a man was with me."[28]

6. So he became obedient to the Father, and came to the wine-press of the cross, which he trod alone. His own arm alone lent him support, according to what we read elsewhere: "I am alone until I pass."[29] Therefore O God, lift him up. Give him that name which is above all names, so that at the name of Jesus, every knee should bend in heaven, on earth, and under the earth.[30] "He has ascended on high and taken captives; he has given gifts to men."[31] What gifts are these? To his Bride, the Church, he left his own robe as a pledge of her inheritance, a many-colored robe, woven from top to bottom.[32] It is many-colored because of the many different orders that are distinguished within it; it is seamless because of the undivided unity of a love that cannot be torn apart,[33] as it is written: "Who will separate us from the love of Christ?"[34] First, hear how the robe is many-colored: "There are varieties of graces, but the same Spirit;

---

26. Gen 37:32.   27. Cf. Eph 4:11f.   28. Is 63:2f.
29. Ps 141:10.   30. Cf. Phil 2:9f.
31. Cf. Ps 68:18; Eph 4:8.   32. Jn 19:23.
33. Cf. *Letter* 334: "The tunic of Christ is the unity of the Church which does not admit of being torn or divided. What has thus been woven, what the Holy Spirit has thus unified, cannot be torn up by men" (PL 537d; trans. James, no. 246, p. 326; cf. *Letter* 219, 2; PL 384a; trans. James, no. 293, p. 360).
34. Rom 8:35.

there are different works, but the same Lord."[35] Then, after listing the various charisms, which correspond to the different hues of the many-colored robe, the Apostle adds the following, to show that it is also seamless, woven from top to bottom: "All these are the work of one and the same Spirit, who apportions to each as he pleases.[36] For love has been poured forth in our hearts by the Holy Spirit, who has been given to us."[37]

Therefore, let there be no division within the Church. Let it remain whole and entire according to its inherited right. Concerning the Church it has been written: "At your right hand stands the queen in a golden robe, interlaced with variety."[38] This is why different people receive different gifts. One man is allotted one kind, one another, irrespective of whether he be a Cistercian or a Cluniac, a regular or one of the laity. This applies to every order and to all languages, to both sexes, to every age and condition of life, everywhere and always, from the first man down to the last. It is for this reason that the robe is described as being ankle-length,[39] since it reaches down to the furthest extremities. "Nothing," as the Prophet says, "is concealed from its warmth."[40] In this way it fits the wearer, since another part of the Bible says of him: "He reaches mightily from one end to the other, he orders all things well."[41]

IV. 7. Therefore, let us all work together to form a single robe, and let this one robe include us all. I say this because, although the components are many and varied, my dove, my fair and perfect one is one only.[42] It is not I by myself, nor you without me, nor a third person on his own, who can form this one robe, but all of us together, provided we take care to maintain the unity of the Spirit in the bond of peace.[43] I repeat, it is not our Order alone, nor yours alone that makes up this unity, but ours and yours together, unless, of course, there be envy and mutual offense.[44] Then we would be

---

35. 1 Cor 12:4f.   36. 1 Cor 12:11.   37. Rom 5:5.   38. Ps 45:9.
39. Gen 37:23.   40. Ps 19:6.   41. Wis 8:1.
42. A combination of Song 2:10 and Song 6:8. The same composite text appears in *De Consideratione*, II, viii, no. 5 (*S. Bern. Op.*, III, p. 423).
43. Cf. Eph 4:3.   44. Cf. Gal 5:26.

devouring each other, and both of us would be consumed,[45] and the Apostle could not unite us to the Husband to whom we have been betrothed; he could not present us as a pure bride to Christ.[46]

In the Song of Songs, the Bride says: "Set love in order about me,"[47] as if to say that though love is one, yet it can be set in order as if it were many. What am I saying? I am a Cistercian myself, but this does not mean that I reject Cluniacs. On the contrary, I am very fond of them; I praise and extol them. You might ask: "Why don't you join them if you think so highly of them?" My reply is this: because, as the Apostle says, "everyone should remain in the vocation in which he was called."[48] If you ask why, in that case, I didn't pick the Cluniacs in the beginning, I would answer that, as the Apostle says elsewhere, "all things are lawful, but not everything is to be recommended."[49] It is not that this Order is not holy and virtuous. The reason is that I am an unspiritual man, sold under sin.[50] I knew that my soul was so weak as to require a stronger remedy. Different remedies are prescribed for different illnesses; the more serious the illness, the more drastic the remedy. Take the case of two men with fever, one with quartan, the other with tertian. The man with the quartan fever might recommend to the other that he take only water, pears, and other cold dishes, whereas he himself has none of these things, but takes wine and hot dishes instead, such

---

45. Cf. Gal 5:15.   46. 2 Cor 11:2.

47. Cf. Song 2:4 (Vulg.): *Ordinavit in me caritatem.* Usually when Bernard speaks of the "ordering of love," *ordinatio caritatis,* he is referring to an alignment of man's affections with God's will, and the consequent exclusion of anything inordinate. It is a question of practical discretion in love, the ability to assess priorities realistically. Cf. Sermon 49, 6, *On the Song of Songs* (*S. Bern. Op.,* II, pp. 75 f., trans. Luddy, II, pp. 60 f.). In the present instance, however, the nuance is different. Noting the various forms of religious life, and perhaps punning on the word *order,* Bernard here touches on a point that he will be covering in no. 8. The unitive power of love does not suppress multiplicity, but integrates or orders it. For a general treatment of the *ordinatio caritatis,* cf. M. Standaert, "Le principe de l'ordination dans la théologie spirituelle de S. Bernard" in *Collectanea O.C.R.,* 8 (1946), pp. 176–216.

48. 1 Cor 7:20; cf. Bernard's *Letter* 32, 3 (PL 138b; trans. James, no. 33, p. 67).

49. 1 Cor 10:22.   50. Cf. Rom 7:14.

things being more suited to his condition. Who could cavil at this? If the second man were to ask: "Why don't you drink water yourself, if you think so highly of it?", wouldn't he be justified in replying: "It is for your benefit that I give it to you; it is for my own that I go without."?[51]

8. It may equally be asked why I don't join all orders, since I praise them all. For it is a fact that I do praise them all, and love any that live good and virtuous lives in the Church. I am attached to all the orders by love, but it is in one alone that I find my work. Yet I trust that my love will so bring it about that I will share also in the fruits of these orders to which I do not belong. I will go even further. You yourself will have to be very careful, for it could happen that your work be fruitless; on the other hand it is quite impossible that my love for your work be so. Oh, how bold is love! One man works without loving, a second man loves without working. The first man's labor is lost, the other man's love will never fail.

Why wonder at this variety during the time of exile, while the Church is on pilgrimage? Why wonder that its unity is also plurality? Probably even in the homeland, where unity will be supreme, there will be different forms of equality. Thus it is written: "In my Father's house there are many rooms."[52] Just as there are many rooms in a single house, so there are many different orders in the one Church. Just as on earth there are different graces, but the one spirit, so in heaven there are different types of glory within a single house. In both cases unity consists in the singleness of love. Here below diversity resides in the differences of orders and the various allotments of work; in heaven diversity will take the form

51. What Bernard seems to be saying is that it is better medicine to treat the cause of illness rather than its symptoms. In the example given, both men are intermittently feverish, but the difference in the cycles of their paroxysms indicates that different causes are operative, and hence that different remedies are required. Hippocrates regarded the quartan as the mildest of all fevers, since it often heralds the recession of more serious disorders (cf. *Of the Epidemics*, I, iii, 2; trans. F. Adams in *Great Books of the Western World*, No. 10 [Chicago: *Encyclopaedia Britannica*, 1952], p. 49).

52. Jn 14:2.

of an obvious and well-ordered gradation of merit. The Church understands this mingling of harmony and discord when it says: "He led me along paths of virtue for his name's sake."[53] Paths is plural, virtue singular, hence neither the diversity of works nor the unity of the workmen is overlooked.

The Church looks forward to this manifold unity, and devotedly sings glad tidings: "The squares of Jerusalem will be paved with pure gold, and all her streets will cry, 'Alleluia'."[54] The squares and the streets may be understood to represent the different crowns and glories. In the gold with which the whole of the city is said to be adorned, and in the single song of Alleluia, you may recognize how alike are the different types of glory, and understand how it is that many minds can be united in a single spirit of devotion.

9. There are many paths that can be taken, for the dwelling-places to which we journey are many. Whatever path a man is taking, let him not be so concerned about alternative routes that he lose sight of his destination.[55] Let him be sure that by following the path he is on, he will eventually arrive at one of the dwelling-places, and will not be left outside his Father's house.

"Star differs from star," says St Paul, "and so will it be at the resurrection of the dead."[56] All the saints will shine like the sun in their Father's kingdom, yet because of differences in merit, some will shine more than others. In the present age, of course, merits cannot be assessed, but in the next, men will be able to judge them easily enough. Here below we see only the works done, there we shall be able to penetrate to the heart, since the sun of Righteousness will reach out in all directions to disclose the hidden depths of hearts. At present, nothing is concealed from its warmth; then, nothing will

53. Ps 23:3.
54. Tob 13:22. Bernard quotes the same version of the text in Sermon 76, 5, *On the Song of Songs* (*S. Bern. Op.*, II, p. 257; trans. Luddy, II, p. 405). Dom Leclercq notes that no trace of this rendering can be found in any of the available Latin versions of Tobias, although the responsory *Plateae tuae* for the third week after Easter is very close to it (*Recueil*, I, p. 306).
55. Lit. "that he deviate from the one virtue." The reference is to the interpretation of Ps 23:3 given in the previous paragraph.
56. 1 Cor 15:41f.

be untouched by its splendor. Judgment passed on the basis of works alone is risky, since it is liable to error; it often happens that those who do the most work have the least virtue. [Here ends my defense.]

AGAINST DETRACTORS

V. 10. It has come to my notice that there are some members of our Order who are speaking unfavorably of other orders, contrary to what the Apostle says: "Do not pass judgment prematurely, before the coming of the Lord. He will light up things hidden in darkness, and disclose the designs of the heart."[57] Instead of submitting to God's justices, such people wish to set up their own.[58] This being the case, they belong neither to our Order, nor to any other. They may live orderly lives, but their haughty language makes them citizens of Babylon, which means "disorder";[59] they are sons of darkness and children of hell, where there is no order but unending chaos.[60]

To you brothers am I speaking, who scorn others and rely on your own virtues, even after hearing the Lord's parable of the Pharisee and the Publican. I have heard it said that you speak of yourselves as the only ones with any virtue, as holier than everyone else, and the only monks who live according to the Rule; as far as you are concerned, other monks are simply transgressors.

11. To begin with, who are you to pass judgment on another's servant? It is before their own master that they stand or fall.[61] Who made you their judges? It is a disorder if you are so proud of your own Order that you fret about the splinters in your brothers' eyes, without bothering to get rid of the log in your own. You glory in the Rule, yet you yourselves don't keep it. You pass judgment prematurely, contrary to the Gospel, and on the servants of another contrary to the Apostle. The Rule itself has to accord

57. 1 Cor 4:5.
58. Cf. Sermon 14, 1, *On the Song of Songs* (*S. Bern. Op.*, I, p. 76; trans. Luddy, I, p. 127).
59. Lit. "confusion." Cf. Sermon 5, 9, *In Dedic.* (*S. Bern. Op.*, V. p. 395).
60. Cf. Job 10:22.   61. Rom 14:4.

with both Gospel and Apostle, otherwise it would be no rule at all, since it would be itself untrue. Listen to this and learn right order, you who violate good order by saying disparaging things about other Orders: "You hypocrite! First remove the log from your own eye so that you will see clearly to take the splinter from your brother's."[62] Do you want to know to which log I am referring? It is the long, large log of pride,[63] which makes you think you are something, when in fact you are nothing.[64] You foolishly rejoice in your own soundness, and notwithstanding the log, you scoff at others because of their splinters. You say: "O God, I give you thanks that I am not like the rest of men, unjust, extortioners, and adulterers."[65] Don't stop now! Why not also include detractors? Detraction is just as much a splinter as the others; how is it that when you list the other splinters so meticulously you say nothing about this? If you think that it is a matter of little or no importance, listen to what the Apostle has to say about it. "Detractors," he says, "will not inherit God's kingdom."[66] God gives this threat in one of the Psalms; from the context we know that it applies to detractors. He says: "I will rebuke you and accuse you to your face."[67] The man who shifts his gaze from himself, and is more interested in others' faults than in his own, will be wrenched back and made to take stock of himself; and it will serve him right.[68]

VI. 12. They retort: "How can these monks be said to keep the Rule? They wear furs[69] and they eat meat[70] and fat.[71] Every day

62. Mt 7:5.

63. Cf. *The Steps of Humility*, IV, 14 (*S. Bern. Op.*, III, p. 27; trans. Webb and Walker, p. 35).

64. Cf. Gal 6:3.   65. Lk 18:11.   66. 1 Cor 6:10.   67. Ps 50:21.

68. Cf. *The Steps of Humility*, XI, 39 (*S. Bern. Op.*, III, p. 46; trans. Webb and Walker, p. 64).

69. Peter the Venerable pointed to the concession of furs as a sign of Cluny's solicitude toward the infirmity of its members (*Letters* IV, 17; PL 328f.). The authorities he adduces in favor of the practice in *Letters* I, 28 (PL 120c) are repeated by Bernard, *infra*, no. 12. However, when Peter came to write the *Statutes*, he restricted the use of furs, rejecting outright whatever appeared expensive or showy, and allowing only sheepskins and goatskins (*Statute* 17, PL 1030).

70. Further on, Bernard seems to indicate that meat was not, in fact, served

they have three or four different dishes, which the Rule forbids,[72] and they leave out the work it enjoins.[73] Many points of their Rule they modify or extend or restrict as they like." This is so; no one could deny it. But look at God's rule, with which St Bendict's regulations agree. It says that "the kingdom of God is within you,"[74] it does not consist in outward things like bodily clothing and food,

---

in the common refectory at Cluny. Two large fish courses took its place (no. 20), or alternatively, those who wanted meat transferred to the infirmary (no. 21). Peter the Venerable penned a scorching denunciation of meat-eating in the Cluniac dependencies (Introduction, p. 18, *supra*). He repeated his prohibition in *Statute* 12 (PL 1029c).

71. The first Cistercians rejected the use of fat as contrary to the Rule (*Ex. Parv.*, XV; PL 166:1507; trans. Larkin, *op. cit.*, p. 262. *Ex. Magn.* I, 20; ed. Griesser, p. 75, l. 25 f.). At the time the *Apologia* was written Cluny allowed fat every day of the year. In the *Statutes* Peter the Venerable prohibited its use on Friday (no. 10; PL 1028 cd), and during advent (no. 15; PL 1030b).

72. Ch. 39 of the Rule allows two cooked dishes at the principal meal, "so that those who cannot eat one, can make their meal on the other." Cîteaux adhered to this stipulation (*Ex. Parv.*, *loc. cit.*). Peter the Venerable argued that if two dishes were allowed because of individual infirmities, then it is all right to give three or four for the same reason (*Letters* I, 28, PL 126b), and the author of the *Riposte* added that a truly temperate man can eat any number of dishes without giving way to gluttony (*op. cit.*, l. 293, p. 317; l. 371, p. 319). The Cluniac in the *Dialogus* maintains that there are really only two dishes served; the extras which charity prompts are not counted (*op. cit.*, col. 1637).

73. Benedict envisages a monk giving about six hours a day to work. A return to manual work was one of the characteristic features of the Cistercian reform (cf. *Ex. Magn.* I, 20; ed. Griesser, p. 75, l. 33), made necessary, perhaps, by the poverty that surrounded the beginnings of the New Monastery. Initially Peter the Venerable had defended Cluny by saying that since work was merely a cure for idleness (Rule, ch. 48), it was not mandatory if monks could fill in their day with some other occupation (*Letters* I, 28; PL 128d). The same position is taken by the author of the *Nouvelle réponse*. Work is only a concession as far as monks are concerned (l. 235, p. 81), an antidote to their weakness in contemplation (l. 175, p. 79; cf. Rule, ch. 48). Later Peter the Venerable based his case on prudential reasons, e.g., work had to be omitted simply because there was no work available that monks could profitably and decently do (*Letters* IV, 17; PL 329d). In the *Statutes*, Peter makes a complete *volte-face*. Work must be found for everybody, he insists, otherwise monks will spend the day gossiping or just dozing in the sun (*Statute* 39, PL 1037a). That Bernard does not treat more amply of work's omission at Cluny may perhaps be ascribed to the *Apologia's* premature conclusion (no. 30).   74. Lk 17:21.

but in man's interior virtues. "The kingdom of God," as the Apostle says, "is not food and drink, but righteousness and peace and joy in the Holy Spirit."[75] And also: "The kingdom of God consists in power, not in word."[76] You cast aspersions on the Fathers because of mere outward observances, while you yourself don't bother about the more important spiritual regulations laid down by the Rule. You gulp down the camel and strain out the gnat.[77] How absurd! Great care is taken to see that the body is clothed according to the Rule, whilst the Rule is broken by leaving the soul naked. A good deal of attention is given to getting a robe and cowl for the body, since a man is not reckoned a monk without them. Meanwhile there is no thought for his spiritual attire, the spirit of prayer and humility.

There are people who go clad in tunics and have nothing to do with furs who, nevertheless are lacking in humility. Surely humility in furs is better than pride in tunics. After all, God himself made clothes for the first man out of animal skins;[78] John the Baptist in the desert wore a leather girdle round his waist;[79] and Benedict himself, in his hermit days, wore animal skins instead of a tunic.[80]

We fill our stomachs with beans and our minds with pride. We condemn rich food as though it were not better to take delicate fare in moderation than to bloat ourselves to belching-point with vegetables.[81] Remember that Esau was censured because of lentils, not meat,[82] Adam was condemned for eating fruit, not meat,[83] and

---

75. Rom 14:17.   76. 1 Cor 4:20.   77. Cf. Mt 23:24.
78. Cf. Gen 3:21.   79. Cf. Mt 3:4.

80. Lit. "the very one who made the regulations about tunics." Benedict's career as a monk was formally initiated by his receiving from the hand of the priest Romanus, the *melota*, a rough sheepskin garment adopted by most of the Eastern monks. Later, when some shepherds spied Benedict moving among the bushes in his *melota*, they thought him some strange sort of wild animal. Cf. Gregory the Great, *Dialogues*, II, ch. 1; trans. Dom Justin McCann (Rugby: Princethorpe Priory, 1941), pp. 12-13.

81. Cf. Sermon 30, *On the Song of Songs* (*S. Bern. Op.*, I, p. 217: trans. Luddy, I, p. 362).

82. Cf. Gen 26:34.   83. Cf. Gen 3:17.

Jonathan was under sentence of death for tasting honey, not meat.[84] On the other hand, Elijah ate meat without coming to grief,[85] Abraham set a delicious meat-dish before the angels,[86] and God himself ordered sacrifices of the flesh of animals.[87]

Surely it is more satisfactory to take a little wine on account of weakness than to quaff down greedy draughts of water, since Paul counseled Timothy to take a little wine.[88] The Lord himself drank wine and was called a wine-bibber because of it.[89] He gave it to his Apostles to drink, and from it established the Sacrament of his Blood.[90] On the other hand, he would not countenance water-drinking at a marriage-feast,[91] and it was at the waters of Meribah that he punished the people severely for their complaining.[92] David too, was afraid to drink the water he desired,[93] and those of Gideon's men who, in their eagerness to drink from the stream, fell on their faces, were considered unworthy for the fight.[94]

What have you to boast about in your manual work? Martha worked as you do and was rebuked, whereas Mary remained still and was praised.[95] Paul says quite plainly that "bodily work is of some value, but spirituality is valuable in every way."[96] The best sort of work is that to which the Prophet refers when he says: "I am in labor because of my grief,"[97] and, "I think of God and I am ravished, and I exert myself."[98] To prevent us thinking that he is speaking of bodily exertion he adds: "And my spirit grows weary."[99] It is spiritual work to which he is referring, since it is the spirit and not the body that is wearied by it.

VII. 13. You may object: "It looks as though you are so concerned with the spiritual side of things that you discredit even those material observances imposed on us by the Rule." No, such things ought to be done, but without neglecting the others.[100] At the

84. Cf. 1 Sam 14:29. 85. Cf. 1 Kings 17:6. 86. Cf. Gen 18:8.
87. Cf. Ex 20:24. 88. Cf. 1 Tim 5:23 89. Cf. Mt. 11:19.
90. Cf. Mt 26:27. 91. Cf. Jn 2:1f. 92. Cf. Num 20:6.
93. Cf. 2 Sam 23:16. 94. Cf. Jud 7:5.
95. Cf. Lk 10: 36f. See note 24 *supra*, p. 39.
97. Ps 6:6. 98. Ps 77:6. 96. 1 Tim 4:18.
100. Cf. Mt 23:23. 99. *Ibid.*

same time, if it happen that one or other element must be left aside, it is better that it be the material. For, just as the soul is more important than the body, so spiritual practices are more fruitful than material ones. But as for you, if you have become so complacent about your bodily observances that you look down on those who cannot follow suit, then it is you who are the real transgressor. You lose your grip on more important things and cling to trifles, whereas Paul tells us to "seek the better gifts."[101] In this matter of disparaging your brothers, humility is lost when you put yourself on a pedestal, and charity when you trample on others, and surely these are the great gifts. You do well when you wear yourself out with all manner of hard work. You do well when, by the austerity of the Rule, you put to death whatever is earthly in you.[102] At the same time it could happen that the man you judge so unfavorably because he has only a little of what is of limited value, i.e. bodily work, may be richer than you in what is of value in every way, i.e. spirituality.[103] Who, may I ask, keeps the Rule better? Surely it is he who is himself better. And who is better, the humble man or the weary man? Surely it is he who has learned from the Lord to be gentle and humble of heart. This is the one who, like Mary, has chosen the better part; and it shall not be taken away from him.[104]

14. If you think that all those who make profession of the Rule are obliged to keep it literally without any possibility of dispensation,[105] then I dare say, you yourself fail as much as the Cluniac.[106] It may be that he is deficient in many points of external observance, but even you can't avoid an occasional fault, and you know, of course, that anyone who fails in a single point is guilty of everything.[107] If, on the other hand, you admit that some things can be changed by dispensation, then it must be true that both you and the

101. 1 Cor 12:31.   102. Cf. Col 3:5.

103. Cf. 1 Tim 4:8.   104. Cf. Lk 10:42.

105. Bernard's own mind on this subject is exposed at length in *Monastic Obligations and Abbatial Authority (infra)*. See also *De Consideratione*, III, iv, 18 (*S. Bern. Op.*, III, p. 445).

106. "The Cluniac." lit. "he."

107. Jas 2:10: "If a man keep the entire law, but fail in a single point, he is guilty of everything."

Cluniac are keeping the Rule, though each in his own way. You keep it more strictly; he, perhaps, keeps it more reasonably.

I don't mean by this that external means can be overlooked, or that the man who does not employ them will quickly become spiritual. Spiritual things are certainly higher, but there is little hope of attaining them or of receiving them without making use of external exercises, as it is written: "It is not the spiritual that comes first but the physical; and then comes the spiritual."[108] Jacob was unfit to win Rachel's longed-for embraces until he had knowledge of Lia.[109] So too we read in one of the Psalms: "strike up a song, and play on the drum."[110] This means, "Take up spiritual things but first make use of physical things." The man in the best position is he who makes use of both as occasion demands, and with discernment.

15. If this is going to be a letter, it is time it came to an end.[111] I have taken up the pen, Father, as you asked, and rebuked those of our monks who have been speaking unfavorably of your Order, and I have, at the same time cleared myself of unfounded suspicion on this count. However, there is something more I must say. Because I have been unsparing with our own monks, it may appear as though I am condoning a number of elements in your Order, which are not to your liking, I know, and which are, in fact, avoided by all good monks. Though such abuses are in the Order, I hope they are not of the Order.[112] No order can have room for disorder, and whatever is disorderly cannot belong to an Order. Hence my objections must be regarded as helping to promote the

108. 1 Cor 15:46. Bernard often quotes this text. Cf. E. Gilson, *The Mystical Theology of St. Bernard* (London: Sheed and Ward, 1955), pp. 37f.

109. Cf. Gen 29:23.

110. Ps 81:2.

111. A lost Marmoutier manuscript mentioned by Mabillon, and dating perhaps from the twelfth century, describes the *Apologia* as made up of two letters, presumably with the break at the end of this paragraph. Cf. Introduction to the critical edition of the *Apologia* in *S. Bern. Op.*, III, p. 67; Leclercq, *Recueil*, I, p. 244; II, pp. 123f.; W. Williams, *St Bernard of Clairvaux* (Manchester University Press, 1953), p. 348.

112. The distinction may be modeled on the Johannine "in the world" but not "of the world"; cf. Jn 17:15f.

Order, rather than as pulling it down. It is not for belonging to the Order that I rebuke men, but for their vices. So it is that I have no fear that those who really love the Order will be upset by what I am going to say. Quite the contrary, they will probably be grateful that I condemn the things which they themselves detest. If anyone is angry with me, this only proves that he has no real love for the Order, since he will not condemn the vices that are ruining it. To him I reply, in the words of St Gregory, that "it is better for scandal to arise than for truth to be abandoned."[113]

[The end of the section "Against Detractors."]

AGAINST EXCESSES

VIII. 16. It is said correctly that it was by holy Fathers that this way of life was organized;[114] they did not abrogate the Rule, they merely moderated its severity on account of the weak, so that more men might be saved. At the same time, I would hate to think that these holy Fathers would have commanded or allowed the many foolish excesses I have noticed in several monasteries. I am astonished that monks could be so lacking in moderation in matters of food and drink, and with respect to clothing and bedding, carriages and buildings. Things have come to such a pass that right order and religion are thought to be promoted, the more concern and pleasure and enthusiasm there is regarding such things. Abstemiousness is

113. Gregory the Great, *In Ezek.* I, vii, 5 (PL 76:842). The same text is quoted in Bernard's *Letter* 34, 2 (PL 140c), and *Letter* 78, 10 (PL 197a). The rubric following was not included in the primitive edition of the *Apologia*; cf. Introduction, *supra*, p. 9.

114. The sanctity of the founders was alleged as a justification of the Cluniac way of life. "If the Order of Cluny were not pleasing to God, then these holy Fathers would hardly have attained heavenly glory" (Letter of Peter of St John to Hato of Troyes in *Petrus Venerabilis, 1156-1956*, p. 50, l. 37). By summoning these very founders as witnesses for the prosecution (no. 23), Bernard shows that he is not attacking the Cluniac ideal, which is "good and holy" (no. 4), but the abuses which prevent its realization, and which Peter the Venerable himself would later try to suppress. "It is not for belonging to the Order that I rebuke men, but for their vices" (no. 15).

accounted miserliness, sobriety strictness, silence gloom. On the other hand, laxity is labeled discretion, extravagance generosity, talkativeness sociability, and laughter joy. Fine clothes and costly caparisons are regarded as mere respectability, and being fussy about bedding is hygiene. When we lavish these things on one another, we call it love.[115] Such love undermines true love. Such discretion disgraces real discretion. This sort of kindness is full of cruelty, for it so looks after the body that the soul is strangled. How can love pamper the flesh and neglect the spirit? What sort of discretion is it to give everything to the body and nothing to the soul? Is it kindness to entertain the maid and murder the mistress?[116] For this kind of mercy let no one hope to receive the mercy the Gospel promises through the mouth of Truth, to those who show mercy: "Blessed are the merciful, for they shall receive mercy."[117] Rather, he can expect that penalty called down by holy Job on those who are cruelly kind. Speaking in prophecy, rather than merely giving vent to his feelings, he said: "May he go unremembered; let him come to grief like a sterile tree." He then shows how such a punishment was deserved by adding: "He feeds the barren childless woman, and does no good to the widow."[118]

17. It is obvious, then, that the kindness of the flesh is inordinate and unreasonable. The flesh is barren and childless, and in the Lord's words "profits nothing."[119] Also, as the Apostle says, "it will not inherit God's kingdom."[120] Such kindness is ever on the alert to fulfill every whim, caring nothing for the sage's sound advice about looking after the soul. "Have mercy on your own soul," he says, "and you will please God."[121] It is a good thing to be

115. A similar list of misnomers is found in *Letter* 1, 4; (PL 75a; trans. James, p. 4).

116. The following section, down to the beginning of no. 18, is not found in the first edition of the text; cf. Introduction, p. 9.

117. Mt 5:7; cf. Bernard's *Letter* 1, 4 (PL 75b; trans. James, p. 4). The text seems to have been quoted fairly liberally by the Cluniacs.

118. Job 24:20f. The same text is quoted in a similar context in Sermon 35, 3, *On the Song of Songs* (S. Bern. Op., I, p. 250; trans. Luddy, I, p. 418).

119. Jn 6:63.   120. 1 Cor 15:50.

121. Eccles 30:24. A favorite text of St Bernard.

merciful to your own soul; it cannot fail to win that mercy which makes you pleasing to God. Any other sort of mercy is cruelty; it is not love but malevolence; it is not discretion but disorder. It feeds the barren childless women, (i.e. it follows the futile fancies of the flesh), while it does no good to the widow (i.e. it does nothing to cultivate the soul's virtues). The soul is indeed bereaved of its heavenly Bridegroom in this life, yet it has from the Holy Spirit the power to conceive and bring forth immortal children. These will, one day, enjoy their heavenly and incorruptible inheritance, provided they are reared by a guardian who is painstaking and devoted.

18. Nowadays, slackness has become so general that it is accepted as the normal thing. It is condoned by almost everyone unquestioningly and in all innocence, though not for the same reasons.[122] Some monks are detached in their use of such things, and so they incur little or no guilt. In other cases simplicity or charity or necessity is the motivation. There are monks who simply do what they are told, and who are quite prepared to act otherwise if they are so bidden. Some monks strive to avoid trouble with those among whom they live. They do not aim at fulfilling their own whims, but at safeguarding the peace of others. Finally there are monks who cannot withstand the majority voice which vigorously insists that such things are all right, and with all its might resists any attempt on the part of right reason to restrict or change anything.

IX. 19. Long ago, when the monastic Order began, who would have dreamed that monks could become so slack? Oh, how far away we have moved from Anthony and his contemporaries![123]

122. Cf. *Letter* 7, 19 (PL 104d; trans. James, no. 8, pp. 37f.).

123. Appeal to the authority of pre-Benedictine monastic tradition was quite usual in early Cistercian apologetics. Cf. *Ex. Magn.* I, 3f.; (ed. Griesser, pp. 50f.); William of St Thierry, *Vita Prima*, I, vii, 34 (PL 185: 247c); Aelred, *Speculum Caritatis*, II, 24 (PL 195:572c). See also L. Bouyer, *The Cistercian Heritage*, pp. 6f, and the letters of Edmund Bishop published under the title "Cluniacs and Cistercians" in *The Downside Review*, 52 (1934), pp. 223–230. The tendency to go beyond the letter of *St Benedict's Rule* indicates perhaps that the primary concern of the first Cistercians was for an integral monastic life rather than the material fulfillment of the regulations of the *Rule*.

If, from time to time, one of them paid a call on another, they were both so avid to receive spiritual nourishment from each other that they forgot all about their meals. Often they spent the whole day with fasting stomachs, but their minds were feasted. This is the correct order of precedence, when the greater in dignity is served first. This is real discretion, when the more important part is more amply provided for. Finally, this is true love, to tend carefully the souls for love of whom Christ died.

As for us, when we come together, to use the Apostle's words, it is not to eat the Lord's supper.[124] Nobody asks for the heavenly bread, and no one distributes it. There is nothing about the Bible or the salvation of souls. Jokes and laughter and chatter are all we hear. At table, while the mouth is filled with food the ears are nourished with gossip so absorbing that all moderation in eating is forgotten.

On meals

20. Meanwhile course after course is brought in.[125] Only meat is lacking, and to compensate for this two huge servings of fish are given. You might have thought that the first was sufficient, but even the recollection of it vanishes once you have set to on the second. The cooks prepare everything with such skill and cunning that the four or five courses already consumed are no hindrance to what is to follow, and the appetite is not checked by satiety. Once the palate is attracted to piquant flavors, ordinary things begin to pall; but if there is question of unusual flavors, desire is as quickly aroused as if the meal had not yet begun. The selection of dishes is so exciting that the stomach does not realize that it is being over-taxed. We turn up our noses at food that is unadulterated, as nature made it, and prefer to mix things together. We set aside their natural, God-given qualities so as to entice excess with hybrid

124. I Cor 11:20.
125. For the literary genre of this passage, cf. Introduction, p. 17. See also Leclercq, *The Love of Learning*, pp. 137f.

B

delicacies. Hunger, of course, has long since subsided; but there is always room for pleasure.

To take a single example: who could describe all the ways in which eggs are tampered with and tortured, or the care that goes into turning them one way and then turning them back? They might be cooked soft, hard, or scrambled. They might be fried or roasted, and occasionally they are stuffed. Sometimes they are served with other foods, and sometimes on their own. What reason can there be for all this variation except the gratification of a jaded appetite? A good deal of care is given to the appearance of a dish, so that the sense of sight is as much delighted by it as the palate. In this way, even when the stomach rumbles its repletion, the eyes can still feast on novelties. The eyes delight in colors, the palate in tastes, but the poor stomach can't see colors, and isn't tickled by tastes. It has to carry everything, and ends up being more oppressed than refreshed.

On drink

21. How can I recommend water-drinking, when we won't countenance adding water to the wine? All of us, because we are monks, seem to have stomach troubles, and so we have to follow the Apostle's advice and take some wine. I don't know why it is that we overlook the fact that it is a *"little* wine" that he recommends.[126] Even so, I only wish we could be content with plain wine, even though it be undiluted. It is embarrassing to speak of these things,[127] but it should be more embarrassing still to do them. If you are ashamed to hear them mentioned, you needn't be too ashamed to amend. The fact is that three or four times during a

126. 1 Tim 5:23. Cf. Sermon 30, 9, *On the Song of Songs* (*S. Bern. Op.* I, p. 218; trans. Luddy, I, p. 363). According to William of St Thierry, Bernard himself, partly because of his digestive ailment, took wine only rarely, and then well diluted: *Vita Prima*, I, viii, 39 (PL 185:250a).

127. In the primitive edition this sentence reads: "It is embarrassing to speak of such things that, had I not seen them with my own eyes, I would scarcely have credited. . . ."

meal, you might see a cup brought in, half-full, so that the different wines[128] can be sampled, more by aroma than by taste. It is not swallowed, but only caressed, since a seasoned palate can quickly distinguish one wine from another, and select the stronger. It is even alleged to be the custom in some monasteries to give the community honeyed or spiced wine on the major feasts.[129] Is this also on account of stomach troubles? As far as I can see all this is so designed to make drink as plentiful and pleasurable as possible. When the monk gets up from table and the swollen veins in his temple begin to throb, all he is fit for is to go back to bed. After all, if you force a man to come to the Office of Vigils before his digestion is complete,[130] all you will extract from him is a groan instead of a tone. So, when I get to bed I bewail my indisposition, not because I have sinned through gluttony, but because I have no room for more.

On those who stay in the infirmary without being ill

22. A funny story,[131] if it be true, told me by several people who can vouch for it, should, I think be mentioned here. They allege that there are hale and hearty young monks who abandon the common life, even though there is nothing wrong with them, and transfer to the infirmary. The Rule wisely allows the use of meat to the sick and to the very weak for the restoration of their strength,[132]

128. The primitive edition reads: " . . . so that the different wines can be sampled and tested, and the best among them selected. It is even alleged . . ."

129. Bernard had already attacked the use of spices and mulse at Cluny in his letter to Robert of Chatillion; *Letter* 1, 11 (PL 77b; trans. James, p. 8). Peter the Venerable condemned the practice in *Statute* 11 (PL 1028). The author of the *Riposte* staunchly defends the principle of giving something special on feast days, saying that it is only human, *humanum est* (1. 590, *op. cit.*, p. 324). St Bernard's attitude is sketched out more fully in Sermon 3, 2, *On Advent* (*S. Bern. Op.* IV, pp. 176 f.; trans. Luddy, *Principal Festivals*, I, p. 24).

130. Cf. *Rule of St Benedict* (hereafter RB), 8:2.

131. In the critical edition no. 22 begins with the last sentence of the preceding paragraph. This whole section, down to the mention of Macarius in no. 23, was added only in the second edition. Cf. Introduction, p. 25.

132. Cf. RB 36 and 39:11.

but these men desire it, not for the recuperation of an ailing body, but for the satisfaction of the whims of unbridled flesh.

I ask you,[133] is it a safe plan, while the enemy attacks and spears and arrows are flying round on all sides, is it a safe plan to act as though the war were ended and the foe defeated, to put down weapons and go off for a leisurely lunch, and then to lie down unarmed for a nap? What cowardice this is, my brave warriors! Your comrades are out wallowing in blood and gore, and here you are enjoying fine food and taking your morning sleep![134] Not for you to spend night and day making the most of your time in these evil days![135] You prefer to spend the long nights fast asleep, while the days you pass in idle chatter.[136] You are like those who cry "Peace" when there is no peace.[137] How is it that the Apostle's fierce reproach leaves you unashamed? He says: "You have not yet resisted to the point of shedding your blood."[138] Why do you not bestir yourself when you hear the terrible thunder of his threat? "If people say, 'There is peace and quiet,' a sudden catastrophe will strike them, as labor comes upon a woman with child, and no escape will be possible."[139]

How subtle is such medicine! It applies the bandage before any wound is inflicted, and it bemoans the limb as yet unsmitten. It massages the spot before it is bruised, and applies soothing ointment where there is no pain, and plaster where there is no abrasion.

23. To distinguish between invalids and those who are well, the sick are bidden to carry a walking-stick in their hands. This is an obvious necessity, for the stick has to support the pretense of illness where there is no sign of pallor or emaciation. Should we laugh or cry at such foolishness? Is this the way Macarius lived? Is it Basil's teaching or Anthony's command? Did the Fathers in Egypt adopt

133. This passage repeats many of the phrases Bernard used in his letter to Robert. *Letter* 1, 13 (PL 79a; trans. James, p. 9).

134. The author of the *Riposte* interprets this phrase as referring to the practice of going back to bed after the Office of Vigils: l. 974f.; *op. cit.*, p. 334.

135. Eph 5:16.

136. Cf. Peter the Venerable's *Statute* 29 (PL 1037a). See note 73.

137. Ezek 13:10.   138. Heb 12:4.   139. I Thess 5:3.

such a manner of life?[140] Finally, did those holy men whom they claim as the founders and teachers of their Order, Odo, Majolus, Odilo and Hugh, did they hold with such things or value them?[141] All these men were saints, and because of this they were in accord with what the Apostle said: "So long as we have food and clothing, we are content."[142] As for us, we are content only if we have all the food we can take, and clothing that is becoming.

On expensive and extravagant clothing

X. 24. Nowadays monks look for clothes that are stylish and will make a good impression rather than for something serviceable to keep out the cold. They don't opt for what is cheap, as the Rule recommends,[143] but for clothes that are of good quality and which look well. Poor miserable monk that I am, why have I lived to see us come to this? The monastic Order was the first order in the Church, it was out of it that the Church developed.[144] In all the earth there was nothing more like the angelic orders, nothing closer to the heavenly Jerusalem, our mother,[145] because of the beauty of its chastity and the fervor of its love. The Apostles were its moderators, and its members were those whom Paul often calls "the saints." It

---

140. Cf. note 123.

141. Odo († 942), Majolus (†994), Odilo (†1048) and Hugh (†1109), respectively the second, fourth, fifth and sixth abbots of Cluny, were considered the chief agents in the development of the Cluniac tradition. See note 114.

142. 1 Tim 6:8.

143. RB 55:7.

144. It was common practice in the Middle Ages to speak of organized monastic life as a continuation of the apostolic community described in Acts. Cf. H. de Lubac, *Exégèse Médiévale* (Paris: Aubier, coll. "Théologie," no. 42; 1959–1961), II, pp. 579f. See also *Ex. Magn.* I, 2 (ed. Griesser, pp. 49f.) and William of St Thierry, *Vita Prima*, I, iii, 15 (PL 185:235d). The idea is very ancient; Cassian knew two versions of it, the Alexandrian (cf. *Inst.* 11, 5 [S.C., no. 109, p. 65]) and the Jerusalem (cf. *Conf.* 18, 5 [S.C. no. 69, p. 14f.]). Cf. A. de Vogüé, "Monasticism and the Church in Cassian" in *Monastic Studies*, no. 3, pp. 19–52. Also G. M. Columbas, "The Ancient Concept of Monastic Life," *ibid.*, no. 4, p. 107.

145. Cf. Leclercq, *The Love of Learning*, pp. 59f.

was their practice to keep nothing as private property, for, as it is written, "distribution was made to each as he had need."[146] There was no scope for childish behavior. All received only as they had need, so that nothing was useless, much less novel or exotic. The text says, "as he had need;" this means, with regard to clothing, something to cover nakedness and keep out the cold.[147] Do you think they wore silks and satins,[148] and rode on mules worth two hundred gold pieces? Do you think their beds had catskin coverlets[149] and many-colored quilts,[150] if distribution was made only as any had need? I don't imagine they would have cared much about the value and color of their clothes. I don't think they would have bothered

146. Acts 4:35.

147. Although there is no manifest verbal dependence, the thought here approaches that of the corresponding sections of Cassian's *Institutes*. "A monk's clothing should simply cover his body, and avoid alike the shame of being naked and danger from the cold. It should not foster the growth of pride and vanity. . . ." (I, i, 2; S.C., no. 109, p. 38).

148. Lit. *galabrunum aut isembrunum*. The following elucidation by Prof. M. M. Postan is appended to David Knowles' article in *Petrus Venerabilis 1156-1956*. It is reproduced here and in note 150 by courtesy of the editors of the volume.

"*Galabruni:* almost certainly means yellowish brown cloth. *Gialla, gallo*, in the sense of yellow is used throughout the dyeing tariffs in pp. 506–507 of A. Doren's *Die florentiner Wollentuchindustrie*. That various colors could combine with brown to give it a tint is shown by the *tinctura de verdebruni* (*ibid.*, p. 519).

Isembruni: This is the most difficult of all, but the balance of probability is that 'isem' is a corruption of a very common Greek name for a thin silk fabric most commonly used for ecclesiastical vestments; *examiton* or *examitum* in Latin. In 1210 the Bishop of Poitiers promised the Abbey of Cluny an annual gift of *examitum* (*Bibl. de l'Ecole des chartes*, 2ᵉ serie, V, pp. 308 sqq.), cited in W. Heyd, *Histoire du commerce du Levant*, p. 699. In that case *isembrun* would be brown *examitum*."

Both of these fabrics were prohibited by Peter the Venerable in the *Statutes*, on the grounds that they were too showy for monks (no. 16; PL 1030c).

149. Catskins were forbidden by Peter the Venerable in *Statute* 17 (PL 1030d). He is especially wrathful toward the custom of importing them (col. 1031a).

150. Lit. *discolor barricanus*. To quote Prof. Postan once again: "*Barricani:* is almost certainly a corruption of *barrochino*, which is a form of *baldochino*, a cloth of levantine origin of silk and brocade: Doren, p. 519, and Heyd, p. 697."

much about them at all. They were far too busy with their efforts to live in harmony, attached to one another and advancing in virtue. So it is said that "the company of believers was of one heart and one soul."[151]

25. Where is this zeal for unity nowadays? We give ourselves over to outward things, and abandon the true and lasting values of God's kingdom, which is within us.[152] Instead we go abroad, seeking some cold comfort from false and empty baubles. Not only has our religious life lost its inner vitality, we haven't even kept up an outward semblance. Look at the habit. It used to betoken humility. Nowadays, I am sorry to say, monks wear it as a sign of pride—so much so that it is difficult to get suitable material locally.[153] A single roll of cloth yields both monk's cowl and soldier's cloak. No one living in the world, no matter how high his position, even though he were a king or an emperor, would mind wearing our clothes, if they were only cut to fashion.

26. "Religion is in the heart," you say, "not in the habit."[154] I agree. How is it then, that when you want to buy a cowl, you have to make the rounds of all the cities, going through every center of commerce, inspecting markets and scrutinizing shops? Everywhere the whole stock must be brought out. You unroll huge bolts of cloth, finger them, examine them, hold them up to the daylight. You reject anything that is coarse or faded, but once something fine and bright takes your fancy, no matter what it costs, you won't rest until it is yours. May I ask whether this sort of thing comes from the heart, or do you do it without thinking? Is it intentionally that you contravene the Rule by seeking out very carefully what is unusual, and therefore more expensive, rather than something cheap? Any vice that shows up on the surface must have its source in the heart. A frivolous heart is known by frivolous conduct, external extravagance points to inward impoverishment, and soft

---

151. Acts 4:32.   152. Lk 17:21.   153. Cf. note 149.

154. The author of the *Riposte* actually does cite this maxim (l. 1313, *op. cit.*, p. 343), but since we do not possess his reply to this passage of the *Apologia* we do not know how he reacted to Bernard's remarks. Cf. *De Consideratione*, III, v, 20 (*S. Bern. Op.*, III, p. 447).

clothes are a sign of a soul without firmness. The fact is that there would not be so much concern for the body, if the fostering of spiritual values had not long since been neglected.

On the negligence of superiors

XI.   27. The Rule states that the superior will be responsible for the wrong-doing of his subjects,[155] and the Lord threatens through the Prophet that he will hold pastors to account for the blood of those who die in their sins.[156] This is why I am astonished that our abbots leave such things uncorrected. Perhaps, if I may say so, the reason is that they are hesitant about blaming others for the things they also do. After all, it is only human not to mind others taking the same liberties one allows oneself. This is what I say; I may be speaking brashly, but it is the truth. Oh, how has the light of the world become darkened, and the salt of the earth insipid?[157] Those whose lives should trace out a path of life for others, give instead, by their behavior, an example of pride. Those who are to lead the blind, have themselves been blinded.[158]

On riding in state

To take a single example: what evidence of humility does it give to go about in such pomp and circumstance, attended by so many retainers that an abbot's suite would be enough for two bishops? If I am not mistaken, I have seen an abbot with sixty horse and more in his retinue. If you saw him ride by you would think he were the Lord of the Manor, or a provincial governor, instead of a monastic father and shepherd of souls. Orders are given for table-cloths and cups and dishes and candle-sticks to be loaded up. Packs are stuffed full, not so much with bedding as with decorative

155. Cf. RB 36:10.   156. Cf. Ezek 5:18.
157. Cf. Mt 5:13f.   158. Cf. Mt 15:14.

coverlets. A man can't go a dozen miles from home without carting all his chattels with him, as if he were going to the wars, or through a desert where the necessities of life are unobtainable. Is it too much to ask that you wash your hands from the same vessel that holds your wine? Do you think that a candle won't burn unless it be mounted on your own silver or gold candle-stick? Will you be sleepless without a parti-colored mattress and an imported coverlet? Wouldn't it be possible for the same servant to act as groom, waiter, and valet? Finally, if we are not able to make do without such a throng of men and beasts, couldn't we at least carry our own supplies with us, so that we don't become a burden on our hosts?[159]

On gold and silver images in monasteries

XII.   28. These are only small things; I am coming to things of greater moment. I merely mention these minor details because they happen to be rather common. I shall say nothing about the soaring heights and extravagant lengths and unnecessary widths of the churches, nothing about their expensive decorations and their novel images, which catch the attention of those who go in to pray, and dry up their devotion.[160] To me they seem like something out of

159. Peter the Venerable restricted a monk's retinue to three (*Statute* 40; PL 1037b). Prof. Knowles thinks that a couple of grooms and valets must be counted in addition ("The Reforming Decrees of Peter the Venerable" in *Petrus Venerabilis, 1156–1956* [Rome: Studia Anselmians, 1956], p. 15). It has been suggested that Bernard is thinking of Suger, the abbot of St Denis, to whom he later wrote: "As for myself, the whole and only thing that upset me was the pomp and splendor with which you traveled. This seemed to savor of arrogance" (*Letter* 78, 3; PL 193a; trans. James, no. 80, p. 112). This is possible, but we have no reason to believe that a taste for the splendid was an uncommon ecclesiastical failing at the time the *Apologia* was written.

160. This example of *praeteritio* is discussed in the Introduction, p. 13. Bernard's contemporaries would have instinctively applied Bernard's remarks to the huge church at Cluny, the largest in Christendom until the building of St Peter's. The building was some 600 feet long, with a width of about 130 feet, divided into five aisles. Its clerestory rose to about 100 feet. During the years immediately following the divulgation of the *Apologia*, from 1125–1130, Peter the Venerable, apparently uninhibited by its strictures, repaired

the Old Testament; but let them be, since it is all to the glory of God. However, as one monk to another, may I ask the question which a heathen poet put to his fellows. "Tell me, O priests," he said, "why is there gold in the holy place?"[161] I shall put the question slightly differently, I am more interested in the sense of the text than in its precise words. "Tell me, O poor men," this is my question, "tell me, O poor men—if you are really poor men—why is there gold in the holy place?" It is not the same for monks and bishops. Bishops have a duty toward both wise and foolish. They have to make use of material ornamentation to rouse devotion in a carnal people, incapable of spiritual things. But we no longer belong to such people. For the sake of Christ we have abandoned all the world holds valuable and attractive. All that is beautiful in sight and sound and scent we have left behind, all that is pleasant to taste and touch. To win Christ we have reckoned bodily enjoyments as dung.[162] Therefore, I ask you, can it be our own devotion we are trying to excite with such display, or is the purpose of it to win the admiration of fools and the offerings of simple folk? Living among gentiles, as we do, it seems that we now follow their example, and do service to their idols.[163]

---

and rebuilt on a grand scale. Cf. Kenneth J. Conant, "Cluniac Building during the Abbacy of Peter the Venerable" in *Petrus Venerabilis, 1156–1956*, pp. 121–127. St Bernard's own ideas on monastic architecture are incarnated in the abbey of Fontenay, Clairvaux's second daughter house, founded in 1118. The church was consecrated in 1147 by Pope Eugene III, and is virtually intact today. There is a series of views of the church, together with some of its history in *L'art cistercien* (Cahiers de la Pierre-qui-Vire, 1962, pp. 66–74, plates 1–14). An older and fuller treatment is Lucien Begule's *L'Abbaye de Fontenay et l'architecture cistercienne* (Lyons: Rey, 1912). Although the church is quite large (approx. 220' × 60' × 55'), it is quite unpretentious in design and very plain in furnishing. But as Abbot Cabrol remarks ("Cluny et Cîteaux" in *S. Bernard et son temps*, p. 27), the time would come when the Cistercians would erect churches far more flamboyant and expensive than anything Cluny produced. A glance at some of the examples of Baroque in L. Lekai's *White Monks* is instructive in this respect.

161. Perseus, *Satires*, II, 69 (*A Persi Flacci et D. Iuni Iuvenalis Saturae*, ed. W. V. Clausen [O.U.P., 1959], p. 11). Cf. Bernard's *De Moribus et Officio Episcoporum*, II, 5; PL 815d. See also Leclercq, *Love of Learning*, pp. 144f.

162. Phil 3:8.   163. Cf. Ps 106:35f.

Let me speak plainly. Cupidity, which is a form of idolatry,[164] is the cause of all this. It is for no useful purpose that we do it, but to attract gifts. You want to know how? Listen to the marvels of it all. It is possible to spend money in such a way that it increases; it is an investment which grows, and pouring it out only brings in more. The very sight of such sumptuous and exquisite baubles is sufficient to inspire men to make offerings, though not to say their prayers. In this way, riches attract riches, and money produces more money. For some unknown reason, the richer a place appears, the more freely do offerings pour in. Gold-cased relics catch the gaze and open the purses. If you show someone a beautiful picture of a saint, he comes to the conclusion that the saint is as holy as the picture is brightly colored. When people rush up to kiss them, they are asked to donate. Beauty they admire, but they do no reverence to holiness. This is the reason that churches are decked out, not merely with a jewelled crown, but with a huge jewelled wheel, where circles of lamps compete in radiance with precious stones.[165] Instead of candle-sticks we see tree-like structures, made of much metal and with exquisite workmanship, where candles and gems sparkle equally.[166] Do you think such appurtenances are meant to stir penitents to compunction, or rather to make sight-seers agog? Oh, vanity of vanities, whose vanity is rivalled only by its insanity![167] The walls of the church are aglow, but the poor of the Church go hungry. The stones of the church are covered with gold, while its children are left naked. The food of the poor is taken to feed the

164. Cf. Eph 5:5.

165. A rather less elaborate version of the *corona* or "crown" will be seen in the foreground of plate 19 in Lekai's *White Monks*. According to Peter the Venerable's testimony, the *corona* at Cluny was really quite splendid. In the *Statutes* he restricts its use somewhat, partly because it was a very expensive apparatus, partly because he felt that its impact was lessened if it was lit up too often (no. 52, PL 1039). The austerity in church furnishing inculcated by St Bernard was traditional in Cistercian churches from the time of Stephen Harding. Cf. *Ex. Magn.*, I, 21 (ed. Griesser, p. 28).

166. Père Anselme Dimier suggests that this refers to the candelabrum which stood at the sanctuary entrance in Saint-Remy at Rheims (*L'art Cistercien*, p. 35).

167. Cf. Eccles 1:2.

eyes of the rich, and amusement is provided for the curious, while the needy have not even the necessities of life.

What sort of respect is shown for the saints by placing their images on the floor to be trampled underfoot? People spit on the angels, and the saints' faces are pummelled by the feet of passers-by. Even though its sacred character counts for little, at least the painting itself should be spared. Why adorn what is so soon to be sullied? Why paint what is to be trodden on? What good are beautiful pictures when they are all discolored with dirt? Finally, what meaning do such things have for monks, who are supposed to be poor men and spiritual? It is, of course, possible to reply to the Poet's question in the words of the Prophet: "Lord, I have loved the beauty of your house, and the place where your glory dwells."[168] Very well, we may tolerate such things in the church itself, since they do harm only to greedy and shallow people, not to those who are simple and god-fearing.

29. What excuse can there be for these ridiculous monstrosities in the cloisters where the monks do their reading, extraordinary things at once beautiful and ugly? Here we find filthy monkeys and fierce lions, fearful centaurs, harpies, and striped tigers, soldiers at war, and hunters blowing their horns. Here is one head with many bodies, there is one body with many heads. Over there is a beast with a serpent for its tail, a fish with an animal's head, and a creature that is horse in front and goat behind, and a second beast with horns and the rear of a horse. All round there is such an amazing variety of shapes that one could easily prefer to take one's reading from the walls instead of from a book. One could spend the whole day gazing fascinated at these things, one by one, instead of meditating on the law of God. Good Lord, even if the foolishness of it all occasion no shame, at least one might balk at the expense.[169]

168. Ps 26:8.

169. Bernard's insistence that monks express the poverty and spirituality of their lives by the austerity of their buildings, is sometimes understood as a blanket condemnation of art. A closer look at this present chapter, however, reveals that Bernard's attitude to church art admits of degrees. He approves of whatever serves a devotional or instructional purpose, and considers bishops

30. There are plenty of other things that could be added, but I am prevented from going on by the burdens of my office, and by your imminent departure, dear brother Oger.[170] You will not agree to stay any longer, and you refuse to go without this latest little book. I shall do as you wish, and let you go, cutting short my words. In any case, a few words spoken in peace will do more good than many

bound to promote it. Secondly, he is dubious about the value of building grandly "for the glory of God," especially when it gives rise to scandal, cupidity or distraction among men. However he is prepared to cede ground here. Finally, he regards as completely inappropraite whatever has merely entertainment value. Grotesques are inexcusable in the cloisters because, apart from being an affront to the poor, they are inclined to distract the monks from their reading. Emile Mâle refers to this passage in support of his opinion that such images, whatever their original signification, were completely meaningless and devoid of any instructional intent by the twelfth century (Cf. *The Gothic Image, Religious Art in France in the 13th century* [London: Collins/Fontana, 1961], pp. 48ff., 60ff.; *Religious Art in France from the 12th to the 18th century* [New York: Noonday Press, 1959], p. 49). To understand Bernard's attitude it must be recalled first of all that he is speaking only of the decoration of monastic cloisters. For the medievals, who centered their lives and values rather profoundly on the sensorium, environment probably had an even greater impact on their moods than it does for us. To sit down to serious reading amid such a riot of amusing images was unthinkable. Bernard's contention that some people would spend the whole day fascinated by the grotesques may very well be less an exaggeration than we would expect. His attitude is echoed by Aelred of Rievaulx. "So in the monastic cloisters we see cranes and hares, deers, stags, magpies and crows. These are not the means recommended by Anthony and Macarius. They are more like the amusements of women. Such things do not accord with monastic poverty; they serve only to entertain the eyes of the frivolous. One who prefers the poverty of Christ to such pleasures of sight does not go beyond the limits of necessity. He would rather build shelters for his poor brothers than construct buildings of such extravagant proportions and unnecessary height. Enter such a one's church and you will find no paintings, no statues, no carpets spread over marble floors. The walls will not be covered with murals depicting pagan legends or royal battles or even scenes from Scripture. There will be no wonderful blaze of candle-light reflected on shining vessels. . . ." (*Speculum Caritatis*, II, 24; PL 195: 572cd; trans. Walker and Webb, *The Mirror o, Charity* (London: Mowbrays, 1962), pp. 74f.).

170. Cf. Introduction, p. 8. Oger was a canon regular of Mont-Saint-Eloi at the time the Apologia was composed. In 1125 he became superior of a new foundation at St Médard in Tournai, and was abbot of this house for fourteen years. His resignation from office provoked Bernard's *Letter* 87 (trans. James, no. 90).

which give rise to scandal. I do hope that these few things I have written will not cause scandal, even though I realize that my condemnation of vices must offend those concerned. Yet, if God so will, it could happen that those whom I fear to vex will be grateful for what I say, and will give up their vices. I mean that the more austere monks will stop belittling others, and that those who have been remiss in the past will put an end to their excesses.[171] In this way both sides can maintain their own values, but without passing judgment on those who think differently. A good man should not be envious of those who are better, and the man who thinks his own course of action good, should not despise a lesser good that another has. The monk who can live austerely should not be harsh toward those who cannot, but at the same time he should avoid modeling his conduct on theirs. Those who cannot live austerely should admire those who can, but they shouldn't imitate them injudiciously. For, just as there is danger of apostasy if a man render less than he vowed, so too, there is danger that those who try to do too much will come to grief.

On Monks who come to us from other Observances and afterwards leave[172]

31. Some monks I have known, who have come to us from other communities and observances, who have knocked and gained admittance, have scandalized their brothers by their thoughtless departure, and have been no advantage to us, upsetting us by their wretched conduct. They scorned what they had, and foolishly coveted what was beyond them. However, by the due outcome of it all, God has made known how worthless they were. Fecklessly they let go of what recklessly they had snatched at, and they

171. That such a statement is included in a hastily written conclusion may indicate that Bernard himself regarded the two parts of the *Apologia* as constituting a single unit, that he is just as serious in his rebuke to detractors as he is in denouncing the abuses of Cluny. Cf. Introduction, p. 27.

172. This problem is treated more amply in *Monastic Obligations and Abbatial Authority*, *infra*, p. 138ff, no. 45ff.

returned discredited to the place they had left with so little fore-thought. The fact is that they had sought our cloisters more because they were dissatisfied with your Order, than from any desire of ours. What sort of monks they were was revealed by their flitting back and forth, from you to us, and from us to you, a scandal to us and to you and to every decent man. I have known monks who, under God's inspiration, have begun bravely, and with his help have bravely persevered. Nevertheless it is always safer to carry on with a good work already begun, than to begin afresh on something we might never finish.[173] I pray that we may all try to do this, in order that, as the Apostle says, "all that we do may be done in love."[174]

This is what I think about your Order and ours. This is the sort of thing I say to our monks, and this is what I say, not about you but to you, as you yourself, and anyone who knows me as you do can best testify. Whatever is praiseworthy in your monks I praise and extol.[175] On the other hand, to you and to my other friends I point out whatever is worthy of reproach, in order that it may be corrected. This is not slander, but candor, and I ask you very earnestly, always to do the same for us. Goodbye.

---

173. This characteristic affirmation of principle has numerous parallels: *Monastic Obligations and Abbatial Authority*, no. 46 (*S. Bern. Op.* III, p. 285; *infra* p. 140); *Letter* 32, 3 (PL 138b; trans. James, no. 33, p. 67); *Letter* 78, 13 (PL 199c; trans. James, no. 80, p. 118); and the letter to a monk who wished to become a hermit published by Leclercq in *Etudes sur S. Bernard et le texte de ses écrits* (Rome: Analecta S.O.C., 1953), pp. 138ff. Cf. Guerric of Igny, Sermon 1, 3 on the feast of St Benedict (*Monastic Studies*, no. 3, p. 4).

174. 1 Cor 16:14.

175. Cf. *Letter* 78, 7: "I am all the more bound to lift up my voice and praise the good when I see it for having boldly denounced former evils or else, were I to cry out against what is evil and say nothing about what is good, I would prove myself a mere backbiter and not a reformer, one who would rather carp at evil than remedy it" (PL 195c; trans. James, no. 80, p. 114).

MONASTIC OBLIGATIONS AND ABBATIAL AUTHORITY

SAINT BERNARD'S BOOK ON PRECEPT AND DISPENSATION

C

INTRODUCTION

S T BERNARD wrote what he called his *Book on Precept and Dispensation* when he was entering his fifties. It seems to have been written between 1141 and 1144.[1] Already the author of many works which enjoyed a wide circulation, he was the founder of more than forty monasteries—daughter-houses of Clairvaux, spread over Europe from Sweden to Spain. Since his authority was recognized in many areas of the life of the Church, he was called upon to settle theological controversies and suppress doctrinal errors, and decide difficult or obscure matters of monastic practice.

Two Benedictine monks of Saint-Père-en-Vallée, near Chartres, sent him a list of questions on monastic observances. In particular they were concerned with the binding force of the Rule of St

---

1. The only chronological evidence to support this conjecture is in Letter 111 of Peter the Venerable to St Bernard where he writes: "Send me, if you would . . . that letter of yours . . . that you sent to the monks of Chartres. . . . I once read it at Cluny but have never since been able to get hold of it to read it again"—ed. G. Constable, *The Letters of Peter the Venerable* (Cambridge, Mass.: Harvard University Press, 1967), I, p. 299. Peter was writing in "late spring or early summer 1144" (cf. *ibid.*, II, p. 172). From March to September 1142 he had been in Spain (cf. *ibid.*, II, p. 262). It is not clear whether or not he had read the *De praecepto* before or after this journey. *De praecepto* will be cited here according to the critical edition by J. Leclercq and H. Rochais, *S. Bernardi Opera*, III (Rome: Editiones Cistercienses, 1963), pp. 243–295.

Benedict. Bernard's reply to them constitutes this treatise, *On Precept and Dispensation*. To understand it we must be conversant with the occasion which gave rise to it. The prologue relates both the circumstances in which it was written and the embarrassment which it caused Bernard.

St Bernard sent this reply to the two monks through the hands of the authority established by the Rule, that is through the hands of their abbot. He then published the treatise along with a covering letter composed at that time. The letter was addressed to the Abbot of Coulombs, in the diocese of Chartres. To him Bernard entrusted the transmission of his work to the monks concerned. Both the prologue and the letter have their interest.

The treatise opens with a perfectly balanced couplet; both lines have the same rhythm, the same number of syllables, the same sounds:

> *Qua mente iam tacebo?*
> *Qua fronte tamen loquar?*[2]

With these questions, this *addubitatio*, Statius, Pliny and other ancient authors have begun their works; as did Paul the Deacon, Sedulius Scottus and others in the Middle Ages. But here it does stand for a hesitation that was real and long. The anonymous questioners—St Bernard has the delicacy not to publish their names —were insistent. They never stopped writing to him—*crebris epistolis*. They forced his hand—*cogitis me*. Unable to escape a difficult situation, Bernard plunged in—*abyssum ingredior*—not knowing where he would come out—*nesciens . . . qua emersurus*. Bernard used these analogies from the perils of the sea again in the prologue. He feared "to run aground." He was going to risk a letter. It would be a long one perhaps, for the questions addressed to him were many. At least might it remain within the limits of a letter!

2. "Can I defer any longer? Yet dare I speak?"—Preface.

But during the writing, the Abbot of Coulombs arrived on the scene. He asked Bernard to prepare his reply for publication, and for this reason to develop his ideas more fully—more than even a long letter would allow. The author, therefore, made his letter into a book and asked that it should be called by the title which corresponded with its content: *On Precept and Dispensation*. This indicates how much Bernard respected the different literary genres and obeyed the rules proper to each: *Liber, si iudicatis, non epistola censeatur*.

What happened at Saint-Père of Chartres? It is difficult to say exactly for St Bernard is very discreet, but from the few references which do escape him it is possible to reconstruct the existing psychological situation. The monks were in difficulties and had appealed to St Bernard as a recognized authority. They wrote two long letters[3] and followed these up with further communications,[4] in each posing a number of questions which were, as St Bernard declared, very knotty and difficult to resolve.[5] Forced finally to replying, St Bernard did so in the form of a letter; but as it grew too long to fit within that classification it became a treatise, a "book" in itself.[6] Since the monks of Saint-Père had written to him without their abbot's knowledge, out of respect for discipline St Bernard did not reply to them directly but through Roger, abbot of the monastery of Coulombs in the diocese of Chartres.[7] The change in literary form which *De Praecepto* underwent in the course of its composition—and for which the author felt himself obliged to apologize—explains the fluctuations in style between the formally systematic and the less rigorously logical; certainly it does not make easy reading.

3. This is evident from the Preface to the treatise.

4. This is evident from the dedicatory letter to the abbot of Coulombs.

5. "So I yield now to your entreaties and take these difficult knots into my hands"—Preface.

6. Cf. Introductory Letter and no. 61.

7. Roger was abbot of Coulombs from 1119 to 1173 or 1174; the abbot of Saint-Père of Chartres was at this time Udo, who held the office from about 1129 to 1150.

Whatever the actual conditions at Saint-Père, it is clear that the community was going through a crisis, and that it was one of obedience. This appears from the questions which the monks put to St Bernard and which he himself reproduced as accurately as he could.[8] The main ones concern the observance of the Rule and may be summarized thus:[9]

Are all the prescriptions of the Rule considered to be of precept, and does their infraction consequently incur damnation? Or are they merely counsels, recommendations, with slight obligation or even none at all? If this last is the case then where is the line to be drawn between the two? The impression given is that in the very "law" which the Rule constitutes, the monks were seeking some way of narrowing the field of a difficult obedience or reducing it to that minimum below which conscience cannot go without sinning.

To this question concerning the Rule itself, there was added another regarding the superior. What is the exact extent of the submission due him? What has he a right to demand and what has one the right to refuse him? Here again, we sense the desire to reduce the scope of obedience due the abbot.

It becomes evident that it is not simply a problem of the ascetical and interior life or of personal growth in virtue, but one of monastic institutional structure. In framing his answer, St Bernard had therefore to turn lawyer and define in juridical terms the relation which obedience creates between superior and subject, assigning to the Rule all the authority which belongs to it in this respect.[10]

Finally, are there degrees of obedience? The purpose of this

8. "Such is as far as I can recall the substance of your main question, if not your exact words"—no. 1. It seems the monks of Saint-Père had proposed their questions in a given order, which Bernard in his reply modified according to the requirements of his own thesis.

9. The questions relative to the Rule are summed up by Bernard in no. 1; the questions relative to transfer, in nos. 44 and 55.

10. The substance of Bernard's reply is to be found particularly in nos. 10–12.

question is made apparent by the very terms of St Bernard's reply.[11] He makes every effort to show that it is the intention, the attitude of will, or better—it is love, that should determine our submission to the authority of God, whose commands are mediated through a superior. Here it is from the moral standpoint and at the bar of conscience that Bernard determines the relative merit of obedience and the relative gravity of its violation, taking into consideration the nature and importance of the command and the uprightness of intention.

The severe and repeated warnings which St Bernard gives to the monks of Saint-Père in this part of the treatise, and his insistence upon the correct and traditional concept of obedience reveal the serious nature of the crisis through which they were passing. He is trying to impress upon them the necessity of submitting to the abbot as to God himself, of not being "scandalized" at him, or doubting God's will simply because his representative is a frail man.[12] St Bernard refutes the objection that it is practically impossible for a monk to save his soul when such a man holds office. This attitude he considers merely indicative of a heart disposed less to a complete surrender of self to God, than to suspicion, criticism and murmuring.[13] In the face of some very impressive arguments he maintains that obedience is always, for man, a sure way to God.[14] This all seems to imply that the monks of Saint-Père were not in agreement with their abbot's government, that they were making things difficult for him, trying to withdraw from his jurisdiction and accusing him of endangering the salvation of their souls by his conduct.

This gives us insight into the other series of questions they had put forth concerning stability and the change from one monastery to another.[15] In dealing with this subject, St Bernard concentrates on only one of the motives then generally admitted as justification for this *transitus*, namely, the "desire for a stricter form of life." He restricts its application, however, to the desperate case of a monastery

11. Nos. 19–43.   12. Nos. 19–21.   13. Nos. 22–24.
14. Nos. 31–34.   15. Nos. 44–51.

where such irregularity prevails as to impede any kind of religious life. But in a well-ordered house he discountenances the possibility of a transfer without the abbot's consent, even if the observances in force there make the manner of living less perfect, provided they are still good and have the sanction of authority.[16] In this way he closes every avenue by which, under pretext of "justifiable" reasons, the Chartres monks might evade their abbot's jurisdiction—not without giving scandal—by transferring to another monastery. St Bernard even seems to imply that their temptation arose from the fact that in their dissatisfaction with the observances of their own house they felt themselves drawn, like others before them, to the Cistercian way of life, then in its full glory.

Finally, one of the last questions Bernard answers is whether, on the death or deposition of an abbot and before the appointment of his successor, a monk could freely leave the monastery of his profession and fix his stability in some other monastery of his choice.[17] This was a debated point at the time. There is still extant a treatise, written at Bec in the mid-twelfth century, dealing with this problem though not resolving it.[18] That this work was familiar

16. On this question of transfer, cf. M. A. Dimier, "S. Bernard et le droit en matiére de *transitus*" in *Revue Mabillon*, 48 (1953), pp. 48–82. With the question of the *transitus* there is closely bound up that of the *fugitivi*, these latter sometimes being regarded as such only in the broad and quite incorrect sense, i.e., because they had attempted to pass to another observance; texts on this subject have been collected together in *Analecta Monastica*, 7 (Studia Anselmiana, 54), pp. 87–145, under the title "Documents sur les fugitifs." Note: any article cited in these notes without the name of the author is the work of the compiler of these notes.

17. Nos. 56–57.

18. The text edited by Martène, *De antiquis ecclesiae ritibus*, I, II, 2; ed. Antwerp, 1736, col. 469–496, and in part re-edited by A. Wilmart, "Les ouvrages d'un moine du Bec" in *Revue bénédictine*, 44 (1932), pp. 34–38. The bibliography relative to this treatise is given in *Analecta Monastica*, 6 (Studia Anselmiana, 50), p. 177, under the title, "Un traité sur la 'profession' des abbés au XIIe siècle." The formula of profession found in the text edited by Martène (and in *Revue bénédictine*, 44 [1932], pp. 37f.) agrees with that attested to in other monasteries of Rouen or the surrounding district, such as Saint Own, (*ibid.*, *Ordo IX*, 467b) and Saint-Georges de Boscherville, (*ibid.*, *Ordo VIII*, 463d). There was at this time a whole series of writings relative to the meaning

to the Saint-Père monks is possible, even probable, Chartres being quite near Normandy. In fact, several of the ideas about obedience which they propose to St Bernard, with regard to the duties and deficiencies of the abbot and change of stability, are identical with those found in the work *On the Profession of Monks*.[19]

In the above treatise the problem is considered under a two-fold aspect: first, in a speculative consideration of the question of human freedom, then a juridical aspect, applying to monks and abbots the pronouncements made by Councils and Popes on the subject.[20] From these sources it emerges that in the cases of irregular election or appointment of a superior, or of an excommunication incurred by him (especially if he obtained office by means of simony),[21] the obligation of continuing to live with him and obey him is suspended. Our Chartres monks, seeing this hypothesis as their only loophole, had raised doubts about the regularity of their abbot's election and declared that they could not, without unending ill-feeling, remain with him.[22] St Bernard unhesitatingly refutes the idea of a transfer

---

and values of the monastic life and profession, following in the wake of St Anselm (these texts are specified in an article entitled "Une court traité de la vie monastique dans l'école du Bec" in *Spicilegium Beccense*, 1 (1959), pp. 477–488) and others; the text published some time ago by A. Wilmart, "Un court traité d'Aelred sur l'entendue et le but de la profession monastique" in *Revue d'Ascétique et de Mystique*, 23 (1947), pp. 249–273, has given rise to some interesting comparisons on the part of A. Squire OP, "Aelred of Rievaulx and Hugh of St Victor" in *Rech. de Théologie Ancienne et médiévale*, 28 (1961), pp. 161–164.

19. Ed. Martène, col. 490–495. It is difficult to say whether St Bernard knew this treatise. It is true that at the beginning of it, 490a, the question is described as "knotty," *nodosa*, reminiscent of St Bernard's words quoted above in no. 5. Bernard and the monks of Chartres could both have had recourse to a common source for a form of speech which best served their purpose. But it is also possible that the substance of the treatise *De professione* became known to Bernard through the monks of Chartres themselves.

20. Ed. Martène, col. 492–495.

21. Cf. the formula of profession of the Canons of Mende which is edited *ibid.*, col. 463b: "I promise to you, the superior of this monastery, and to your successors canonically installed, due obedience and reverence according to the canonical rule of this holy Order. . . ."

22. No. 56.

occasioned by the death of the abbot, demolishes their argumenta-
tion by quoting Proverbs 18:1: "None so quick to find pretexts as
he that would break with a friend." He refers them back to Matthew
23:3, used in Chapter 4 of the Holy Rule: "Do what they tell you,
but do not follow their practice."[23]

From the accumulated evidence we may legitimately make some
generalization about the situation and the feelings of the monks at
Saint-Père. They objected strongly to the government, too
dictatorial perhaps, of their abbot. They were discontented and
irritated; worse, in their intense resentment towards their abbot
they scrutinized his every action and decision to find a pretext
against him. They imputed authoritarian tendencies to him and
tried to discover in the Rule and in similar documents grounds for
questioning his decisions. They even reproached him for having
neglected, in his government, the good of their souls, upon which
the Rule lays such emphasis.[24] In short they were completely at
odds with him and refused to obey him, or at least, did not do so
wholeheartedly and with a good will. In their attempt to preserve
for themselves a certain liberty, they endeavored to limit the power
of their superior by appealing to the laws then in force, and so to
set their own conscience at rest. Going still further, they thought
they could escape from their abbot by a transfer—unless, indeed,
the root of the whole affair was that they wanted to change to the
Cistercian observance.[25] On this last point the texts do not allow of
any certain conclusion, but the fact remains that the monks did
appeal to St Bernard, saying they knew that his writings and
eloquence could be very influential in a case like this.[26] And in fact,
not only had he already effectively influenced many churchmen
by his interventions, his teaching and actions, but he also understood

---

23. *Ibid.*

24. "He should know that he has undertaken the care of weakly souls, not
a tyranny over the strong" (Rule of St Benedict [hereafter RB], 27:6).

25. Cf. nos. 46–51 where the Cistercian observances are compared with
those of traditional monachism from the point of view of transfer.

26. Cf. Preface.

the problem of monks, entered into their difficulties and identified himself with their cause.[27]

This then was the very real and human situation in which Bernard intervened. In doing so, he was to give a great impetus to the development of the ideas involved, especially in regard to two matters which we should now consider: obedience to the Rule and profession.

Obedience to the Rule of St Benedict

It would seem that the crux of the matter is the precise meaning to be attached to the formula by which the monk promises his obedience "according to the Rule of St Benedict"—*secundum regulam S Benedicti*. Here, for St Bernard, is the decisive point. But this formula is itself the result of an evolutionary process, and some knowledge of this is necessary to grasp the full significance of the formula.[28]

In Chapter 58 of the Rule, where he dealt with "The Manner of Receiving the Brethren," St Benedict had no intention of establishing a formula of public, juridical engagement, precise, detailed and definitive; he simply wanted to show the novice what is expected of him when he was admitted into the monastic community. Nor

27. This is evident from St Bernard's Letter 67, no. 2, PL 182:176, trans. B. S. James, *The Letters of St Bernard of Clairvaux* (London: Burns & Oates, 1953); Letter 70, no. 2, p. 96, and his other letters concerning transfer, and also the fragment *Rem similem* from Letter 70, PL 182:183, note 204, trans. James, Letter 73, no. 2, pp. 102 f. Indications as to the authenticity of this last are to be found in the article, "Lettres de Mabillon et de Rancé sur S. Bernard" in *Revue Mabillon*, 45 (1955), pp. 29–34.

28. There will be no question here of retracing in detail the history of obedience, but simply of giving some indication of the stages of this history in order to place St Bernard in his historical context. Further indications will be found in the two works used here: I. Herwegen, *Geschichte der benediktinischen Professformel* (Münster, 1912) and C. Capelle, *Le voeu d'obéissance des origines au XIIᵉ siècle* (Paris, 1959). As for St Bernard's own teaching supposed or expounded here, it is found particularly in nos. 9–12 (on the limits of profession) and nos. 44–49 (on the relationship between the various ways of following the Rule of St Benedict) as well as in other places, notably in nos. 1–8 (general idea of "precept" and "dispensation").

did he claim to impose several distinct vows, conceived in the manner of what were later to become the "vows of religion"; he was simply stating the scope of the monk's promise.[29] However, he did in fact create a form of engagement to which later monastic formulas would conform. He himself, when speaking in this same chapter of the manner of testing candidates and warning them of what they are to expect, returns almost with insistence to the Rule as a "law" which they must observe; yet he does not actually make mention of it in the "promise." But more and more in the course of the following centuries one made profession "according to the Rule."[30]

To grasp the exact meaning of the phrase *secundum Regulam*, we must bear in mind that it dates from the period sometimes referred to as that of the *regula mixta*. It originated in Burgundy where very early the two streams of monastic tradition—Celtic monasticism and the Rule of St Columban on the one hand and the Rule of St Benedict on the other—met and fused. The purpose of the words "according to the Rule," is to define, at least in general terms, which of the various forms of monastic life the monk has chosen to follow. It indicated the particular prescriptions by which he intends to practice conversion of manners, knowing that they will teach him what he must do to attain purity of heart. This form was more and more directed to the Rule of St Benedict. Not that it was the only Rule then observed in these places; rather, its prescriptions had been adapted to the customs and needs of each monastery.

The reform undertaken by Charlemagne and pursued under Louis the Pious by St Benedict of Aniane sought the exclusive establishment in all monasteries of the Rule of St Benedict.[31] It

29. Cf. B. Steidle, *The Rule of St Benedict*, trans. U. Schnitzhofer (Canon City, Colo.: Holy Cross Abbey, 1966), pp. 251ff.; Capelle, *op. cit.*, pp. 98 and 103.

30. *Secundum Regulam*—for the history of this formula up to the eighth-ninth century, cf. *Recueil d'études sur saint Bernard et ses écrits*, III (Rome: Edizioni de Storia e Letteratura, 1968), pp. 275–278.

31. Herwegen, *op. cit.*, pp. 57–64, and J. Semmler, *Legislatio Aquisgranensis*, C.C.M., I, pp. 425–428.

became the subject of valuable commentaries.[32] Every effort was made to relate all the observances to its letter and spirit. Yet practices inherited from the preceding centuries were still preserved, though an attempt was made to breathe a new spirit into them. Hildemar reverted to the triple formula of profession (stability, *conversatio morum*, which became *conversio morum*, and obedience), already adopted in several places.[33] Into this formula Smaragdus and Hildemar both introduced the phrase "according to the Rule,"[34] and here it was indicated that the Rule of St Benedict should be for the monk the one law having any claim upon him; all his ideas, intentions and activities should conform to it. True, St Benedict of Aniane and those who followed in his footsteps interpreted the Rule in their own way; they were influenced by a tradition already blended with, not to say contaminated by, elements which were quite foreign to ancient monasticism as portrayed in the Rule of St Benedict. But it was at least their intention to return to the Rule, and they strove to adapt everything to the type of observance they themselves created and believed to be authentic. It was this form of observance, derived in fact from various traditions, which in the succeeding centuries was preserved among those soon to be known as the "black monks" to distinguish them from the monks of the newly-founded orders, particularly the Cistercians.

The Cistercians, following the intuition and firm convictions of their first fathers, adhered to the Carolingian concept of the authority of the Rule. They held the commentary of Smaragdus in high esteem, and the formula of profession which they adopted is identical with his.[35] They frequently transcribed St Benedict of

32. Those of Smaragdus of Saint-Mihiel (ed. PL 102:689–932) and Hildemar, both edited together under the latter's name by R. Mittermuller (Ratisbon, 1880), and under the name of Paul the Deacon in "Bibliotheca Casinensis," IV, *Florilegium Casinense* (Monte Cassino, 1880), pp. 3–173; the various recensions have been studied by W. Hafner, *Der Basiliuskommentar zur Regula S. Benedicti* (Münster, 1959).

33. E.g., at St Gall towards 850; Herwegen, *ibid.*, pp. 33–41, 60–61.

34. Cf. Herwegen, *ibid.*, pp. 41–46 and particularly p. 59.

35. This fact was pointed out by Herwegen, *ibid.*, p. 64, according to the formula of profession reproduced by Martène, *Regula commentata*, c. 58, PL 66:820d, under the title: *Formula Cisterciensium*.

Aniane's *Penitential*.[36] Yet they interpreted the expression "according to the Rule" more strictly than it had hitherto been interpreted; for them it meant doing everything in strictest accordance with the purity of the Rule: *puritati regule . . . Rectitudinem regule supra cunctum vite sue tenorem ducentes*.[37] It was within this tradition originated by them that St Bernard was to find his place; he developed it into its fullest expression by making the Rule the norm of monastic obedience and showing that it is the Rule which the monk by his profession pledges himself to observe.

Profession

St Bernard's teaching on this point is scattered throughout several of his writings, though it is principally to be found in this work *On Precept and Dispensation*.[38] When endeavoring to make a synthesis which St Bernard himself never made, there is danger of introducing an artificial or arbitrary relationship. But as will be seen, there is an inner logic uniting all the elements of his thought which the various texts offer, and provided we are careful to restrict their meaning to what they actually say, we can grasp this thought without distorting it.

Faithful to the tradition he had inherited, St Bernard always tries to resolve the problems connected with the obligations of monastic life in terms of the monastic profession. This is particularly the case when it concerns obligations contracted in the matter of obedience. St Benedict established a "school of the Lord's service" for cenobites, where, by living "under a Rule and an abbot,"[39] they were afforded

36. In evidence of this there are the texts quoted in "Les cisterciens et S. Benoît d'Aniane" in *Analecta Sacri Ordinis Cisterciensis*, 7 (1951), pp. 63–64.

37. *Exordium parvum*, c. XIV, ed. J.–B. Van Damme, *Documenta pro Cisterciensis Ordinis historiae ac juris studio* (Westmalle: Typis Ordinis, 1959), p. 13. On the meaning of the formula cited here, cf. P. Stevens, "Rectitudo Regulae" in *Collectanea Ordinis Cisterciensis Reformati*, 9 (1947), pp. 131–142, and P. Salmon, "Monastic Asceticism and the Origins of Cîteaux" in *Monastic Studies*, 3 (1965), pp. 119–138.

38. Nos. 9–10.

39. RB, Prol., 45; 1:2.

the opportunity of amending vice and growing in charity and in purity of heart. By this he did not make obedience merely a form of asceticism whereby the monk submits himself to the spiritual direction of an abbot, and commits himself to his care in all temporal matters. He went further and raised it to the level of a clearcut, juridical relationship existing by God's authority between the disciple and a master who holds the place of God in his regard. Such a relationship is contracted at profession and imposes obligations on both disciple and master, as well as sanctions on God's part.[40]

How does St Bernard conceive this double relationship with the Rule and with the abbot which obedience creates and what precise force does he attribute to the Rule in this sphere? In the texts where he is speaking clearly and explicitly of this,[41] it would seem that he considers the Rule as the very foundation of this relationship of obedience; from it all the other obligations of the monk derive. He is not speaking, here in this treatise and elsewhere, to novices who need instruction in obedience but to monks already formed by monastic discipline, monks who already know their Rule. He does not waste time then demonstrating and explaining ideas which he may presume to be admitted, even if their actual implementation gives rise to difficulties; neither does he define the nature of obedience, nor explain its role in monastic life and how its various components are to be reconciled.

He has, nevertheless, clear-cut views on the subject of the relationship existing between Rule and abbot. This can be discerned in the argument he occasionally employs when reminding abbots of their powers and obligations with regard to the Rule; the abbot can sometimes dispense from it, but can never administer it according to his own will. On the contrary, it is the Rule of St Benedict that determines exactly when the subject must obey and when the

---

40. RB 58:17–29; cf. Capelle, *op. cit.*, pp. 89–94; Rothenhausler, *Zur Aufnahmeordnung*, pp. 2–18 and 95.

41. *Letter* 7, no. 17, PL 182:103, trans. James, Letter 8, p. 36; *Letter* 7, no. 4, PL 182:95–96, trans. James, p. 28; *Sermones de Diversis*, 41, PL 183:653–661. It is evident from these and other texts that Bernard had a complete doctrine of obedience, but that he never expressly formulated it or synthesized it.

abbot can command. In other words, the Rule is the norm of obedience, the "principle" norm, in the original sense of the word. It is the beginning, the origin, of all acts of obedience, and they derive from it as from a "principle." St Bernard indicates this with reference to the observances prescribed by St Benedict.

> I would say that these sacred observances have been entrusted to the prudence and integrity of superiors, not made subject to their will.... For surely the profession by which a young monk subjects himself to a superior is equally binding on the superior? To my mind they are equally bound by a common promise, for by the solemn engagement of the one, both have become debtors mutually, the one owing humble obedience and the other a sincere and fatherly solicitude.... The one who makes profession does indeed pledge himself to obedience; not just any kind of obedience, however, but explicitly obedience "according to the Rule," and to no other Rule than that of St Benedict. The superior, then, cannot allow his will free rein over his subjects, he must understand that its scope has been determined *by the Rule*. His commands should be confined solely to what is right—not right in a general way, but according to what St Benedict has established. And so the profession runs: "I promise . . ." what? the Rule? No, but "obedience according to the Rule of St Benedict." Supposing then that I make profession according to that Rule, and my abbot tries to impose on me something that is not according to the Rule, is there, in this case, any need for me to submit? I would say that he can demand of me only what I have promised.[42]

This passage reveals St Bernard's view of the relationship of obedience existing between the monk and the spiritual father to whose guidance he has committed himself. This mutual relationship created by the voluntary engagement of the monk's profession is based entirely upon the Rule of St Benedict, and it is the Rule which determines its full meaning and scope. When the monk promises to obey "explicitly," *determinate*, according to the Rule of St Benedict, he is by that very fact declaring his intention of following the Rule as the path which will lead him to God. He determines

42. No. 10.

to adapt his behavior, which must from now on be governed by the law of obedience, to everything St Benedict prescribes and to that alone. This intention forms the basis of the contract by which he surrenders his will into the hands of an abbot. He desires to obey simply because he will find, without doubt or delay, uprightness of life and union with God. In view of this goal which he means to attain through his profession, he makes the observance of the Rule of St Benedict the object of his obedience; it is the Rule that gives to this obedience what might be called its specific character. Although St Bernard does not use these precise words, taken as they are from a language not his own, they do correspond to his thought. For his teaching is that the entire matter of obedience is determined by the Rule and that obedience should be exercised according to the Rule and in no other way. It is the Rule which determines not only the nature of obedience but also its extent and manner of execution.

The abbot who receives the profession is one of the two parties between whom the relationship of obedience is exercised. He has the obligation, by reason of the very promise made by the monk to observe the Rule, to use every means—commanding, teaching, reasoning, leading and if need be even pressing him into these acts of obedience—to assure that the monk fulfills his vow. By the authority which he possesses (which is "executive" rather than "legislative"), the abbot's duty to his monks is to help them fulfill their obligations towards the Rule and to reprove them should they fail to do so: *adjutor adimpletionis at vindex praevaricationis*. The monks have of their own volition taken this Rule upon themselves as the law which is henceforth essential to their life, and the abbot has been the witness to this engagement:

> In the presence of the abbot as a witness, but not at his bidding as a despot, they are professed before God and his saints; and if they ever act otherwise they stand condemned out of their own mouth, as it were, before him whom they have mocked.[43]

43. *Letter* 7, no. 17, *loc. cit.* Cf. also no. 2, *infra*.

G

This text seems to imply that the abbot's role with regard to the individual monk's obedience is assigned to him by the Rule, for it quotes directly from the Rule's prescription for the rite of profession.[44] It might well be suggested therefore that for St Bernard, the abbot and the monk who obeys him posit the same act, and both of them become executors of the same "law of God," which is none other than the law of charity. In this sense too they become the executors of a "common will,"[45] for together—the one in commanding and the other in submitting—they accomplish a single act with a single object, imposed on each of them by the Rule. So it is the Rule that decides the conduct of each. It is, in fact, the basic norm of monastic obedience since it determines the very *nature* of this obedience.

But the Rule equally determines the *object* of monastic obedience. St Bernard specifies the cases in which the monk must obey in the phrase: *id quod sanctus pater Benedictus instituit*—that which our holy father St Benedict instituted.

The Rule not only provides the foundation for the monk's obligation of obedience, it also defines the limits within which he must exercise this obedience and his right to see them respected by his superior. That is why, in the text quoted above, it is the Rule which is prescribed before all else as the norm for the abbot. On him falls the principal responsibility in the exercise of obedience, because it is only through his exercise of authority that obedience can exist for the monk. But the measure and extent of the matters which he can and should impose are prescribed by the Rule; and in such a way that everything else, however legitimate and useful it may be, is excluded from this field and cannot be prescribed as of obligation in virtue of obedience. Anything not included in the Rule, anything that does not derive from it, was not the object of the promise which constituted profession and formed no part of

44. RB 58:18: "before God and his saints."

45. On the theological context in which such expressions receive their fullest significance in St Bernard, cf. P. Delfgaauw, "La nature et les degrés de l'amour selon S. Bernard" in *S. Bernard Théologien, Analecta Sacri Ordinis Cisterciensis*, 9 (1953), pp. 235–251.

the intention of the contracting parties. In consequence it remains
outside the scope of any obligations the abbot may impose upon
the professed in virtue of their mutual engagement.

When St Benedict requires of the abbot "that he himself keep
the Rule in all things"[46] he is pointing out to him the object of the
obedience of his monks. The actual matter of this obedience is
entrusted to his conscience and prudence. In this way he is the
custodian of obedience and, even if he can in certain circumstances
dispense from it, he should defend it by means of sanctions whenever there is an infraction. But he can never arrange it to suit himself, he can never assume the right to extend or restrict the sphere
of obedience in a way not conformable to what has already been
promised and accepted. He must obey in virtue of his monks' very
obedience, with a view to this obedience. Although the abbot is
himself in some way a norm for his subjects because of the authority he possesses he is not thereby above the Rule (*supra Regulam*).
He too has freely submitted to it by his profession; though
appointed a superior (*praelatus*) he remains a monk.[47] Henceforth
it is his duty to build with obedience the bridge leading both
himself and his monks to salvation.[48] The Rule then is an objective
norm, independent of any man's capricious interpretation, inviolate
within certain limits and having a value both in itself and for all
bound to it.

In practice a certain amount of initiative is left to the abbot whose
duty it is to see that the Rule is observed; he must exercise discernment, make decisions. But the Rule remains the *primary* norm and
in relation to it the other norm—the superior—is secondary and
dependent upon it. For the monk, the abbot's will has the force of
law, but it must always be in conformity with the prescriptions of
the Rule, which is the law for the abbot. The abbot has no right
to exact obedience upon any matter or in any way not preordained
by the Rule. Though in actuality the obedience promised to the

46. RB 64:7-22.
47. *De Moribus et Officio Episcoporum*, 33, PL 182:830ff.
48. *Sermones de Diversis*, 35, no. 6, PL 183:636ff.

abbot by the monk at profession has profound importance, on the juridical level it is secondary.

These ideas drawn from this treatise are supported by what St Bernard once wrote to the monk Adam who, under pretext of obedience, had illicitly left his monastery in company with his abbot.[49] Bernard reminds him that when he pronounced his vows at profession, the abbot was present simply as a witness; the promise was made to God rather than to the abbot:

> Is it into the hands of the abbot that I place what I have un-reservedly affirmed with my lips and signed with my own hand in the presence of God and the saints, knowing from the Rule that if I ever act otherwise, I shall be condemned by him whom I mock? If my abbot, or even an angel from heaven, were to command something contrary to this, I would unhesitatingly excuse myself from an obedience of this kind which would make me break my vow and perjure the name of God. For I know that it is out of my own mouth that I am to be either condemned or justified. . . . Otherwise what a shameless lie it would be to sing that verse of the psalm before God and his angels: "I will pay you my vows, which my lips have uttered."[50] Accordingly, my abbot should reflect on the duty imposed upon him by those words addressed in a special way to him by the Rule: that he should keep this Rule in all things. He should also reflect on what is prescribed for everyone without exception, namely, that all should follow this Rule as mistress in all things and that no one should rashly deviate from it.[51] I resolved then always and everywhere to follow my abbot as master in such a fashion that I should never in any way deviate from the teaching of the Rule which, with him as witness, I have sworn and determined to keep.[52]

---

49. *Letter* 7, no. 17, *loc. cit.* On the circumstances surrounding this affair, cf. L. Grill, "Morimund soeur jumelle de Clairvaux" in *Bernard de Clairvaux* (Paris, 1953), pp. 125–132.

50. Ps 65:13–14 (Vulgate).   51. RB 3:7.

52. *Letter* 7, no. 17, *loc. cit.* In no. 19 of this treatise Bernard explicitly states that the abbot must be regarded as truly holding the place of Christ in the monastery and that he is to be obeyed as Christ himself, provided that he enjoins nothing contrary to the commands of God; if he does, the monk must, following St Peter's example, obey God (Acts 5:29). Cf. *Letter* 7, no. 3,

It would be hard to find a clearer or more emphatic expression of the fact that the Rule is a supreme norm which governs with equal force both the intention and the obligation of the monk and the conscience and administration of the abbot. Here again is evidence that profession according to the Rule creates a double relationship of obedience: firstly with God (this is the primary, principal and fundamental relationship, the direct and personal bond, which imposes upon the monk the full responsibility of remaining submissive to God's will by means of the Rule which reveals it to him); and secondly with the abbot, who acts as intermediary between the Rule and the monk.

The abbot may in practice exercise a more direct mediation and appear to play the principal role. In reality he is dependent upon the Rule and upon the obligation which, according to the Rule, he and his monks have contracted toward God. It is because the first obligation creates a responsibility of a personal nature that the monk has the power and sometimes the duty of refusing obedience, should the abbot enjoin something contrary to the Rule. This refusal would then be a form of obedience. The second relationship—the bond with the abbot—arises from the fact that at profession he acted as witness and representative of the invisible God. He must continue to play this "vicarious" role, helping the monk to prove his fidelity to their common obligation towards God and the Rule. In this way everything should converge towards subordination to the Rule, the mediator between God and the monks. It is in fulfillment of the Rule that God's will, manifested in its precepts, is united with man's action, which in its turn is guided by the prescriptions of St Benedict and so aligned and made conformable to the will of God.

Here, in the last analysis, is the foundation for the authority of the Rule. God intended that his will, proclaimed in the precepts and

---

loc. cit. In the well-documented study, *La promesse d'obéissance ou la "professio regularis"* (Westmalle: Typis Ordinis Cisterciensis, 1955), C. Bock makes no reference to St Bernard for the simple reason that he never mentions a promise of obedience distinct from profession.

counsels of the Gospel, should be interpreted for monks by St Benedict in precise, concrete, practical and relevant terms. It is true, as St Bernard recognizes, that the Rule contains divine commandments, "spiritual" in character, for example charity, humility and gentleness, prescribed by God rather than by St Benedict. It includes also human means of a more "natural" character, such as the "corporal observances."[53] But St Bernard is convinced and in fact teaches that these prescriptions which are of human institution are in perfect accord with God's will. Consequently, they can be observed with the fullest confidence by St Benedict's disciples, as so many sure means leading to God:

> There can be no doubt as to the true holiness of this way of life which was designed by divine inspiration and wisdom rather than by human prudence or ingenuity. It is surely for this reason that Benedict attained a peak of holiness in life as great as was his glory and happiness after death.[54]

The Rule then, though of divine inspiration, also comprises prescriptions of human institution, and these will always be conditioned by and adaptable to temporal circumstances. They are not infallible even though they are in themselves well-fitted to lead the monk to God. But for the accomplishment of God's will a certain discretion will be necessary at times to decide which of them are to be observed and in what way. Not everyone, however, has an equal right to exercise this discretion. The right belongs to those who have been prepared by God for the office of superior by the special gift when their election calls them to exercise it. So it is for God's sake that superiors must be obeyed. It is this consideration, or rather, this view of faith that bestows on the obedience given to a fellow human its true place and value in the religious life.

St Bernard frequently returns to this point, and clarifies it by

---

53. Nos. 2–3.

54. *Declamationes de colloquio Simonis cum Jesu ex verbis S. Bernardi*, 45, PL 184:462. On the authenticity of St Bernard's authorship of this text, cf. *Recueil d'études sur s. Bernard*, I (Rome: Edizioni de Storia e Letteratura, 1962), pp. 16–20.

showing that there are three kinds of precepts. The first are those commands which are purely and essentially good, *pura bona*, such as the exercise of faith, hope and charity, or the Decalogue: "It can never be right to neglect them even though one be forbidden to practice them. Next there are those things which are essentially evil, *pura mala*, that is to say, contrary to those first precepts and like things. It can never be right to do these things even though one be commanded, and here obedience to men can never be enforced." In all these matters which are enjoined or forbidden by the commandments of God, "He is to be given an obedience which no human authority may lessen, an obedience which must be maintained inviolable. It may be held for certain that we cannot, at the will of the superior, either cease to do what is good (those things which are prescribed) or do what is evil (those things which are forbidden)." However, between these two there is another category:

> Between these two extremes there is an intermediate class: things which in themselves are neither good nor evil, but become so according to the circumstances of place, time, manner and person; examples are fasting, reading, vigils, etc. In consequence it can be either good or evil to command or forbid them. But among them, like the tree of good and evil which stood in the midst of Paradise, stands the law of obedience. And in all these matters we must be submissive and obedient to the will of the superior, asking no questions for conscience sake, for none of these things has God preordained as obligatory. He has rather left them to be decided by the superior's authority. This is the kind of obedience which we, who are under a man, owe to a man. It is also a bond between God and man, for whenever obedience is given to superiors it is given to him who says: "He who hears you, hears me."[55]

Instead of each individual exercising discretion as to what should be observed in the last grouping, it belongs to the abbot to exercise this discretion. By so doing he acts as a bridge or a ford which enables the monk to avoid dangerous waters.[56]

---

55. *Letter* 7, no. 4, *loc. cit.* Cf. also *Sermones de Diversis*, 41, no. 3, PL 183:655.
56. *Sermones de Diversis*, 35, no. 6, PL 183:636f.

But as such discretion is so rarely found on earth, let the virtue of obedience be your substitute for it, then you will never do anything either more or less than you are commanded.[57]

There is then no opposition between the obedience due to the Rule and that due to the superior. They unite, complement and condition each other. Both derive from the promise made at profession to obey according to the Rule. This was made principally with God, but also with the superior who represents him and who himself undertakes to observe the Rule and to have it observed. The authority of the Rule then, from the ascetical as well as the juridical viewpoint, finds its basis and its justification as a means of sanctification and a juridical norm.

This doctrine finds a particular application in the special case of a dispensation. To what extent can an abbot dispense from the Rule? This question calls for a study of its own. The answer is necessarily complex and must be carefully nuanced. Here we can only make a few pertinent remarks.

First of all the idea expressed by the *dispensatio* is broader than that contained in the English word, dispensation, which indicates primarily a legitimate infraction of a law by an authority who has the power to do this. In the traditional terminology of Canon Law it refers to any exception or modification, anything from complete abrogation to a particular dispensation, as we commonly understand it today.[58] Yvo of Chartres, who wrote in the period just before Bernard, insisted on the immutability of the divine law, especially as it had been promulgated in the Gospel. At the same time he held that all human law, which is only to be an application of the divine law, is subject to dispensation.[59] Bernard's treatise is

---

57. Sermon for the Octave of the Feast of the Circumcision, no. 11, PL 183:142, trans. A. Luddy, *St Bernard's Sermons for the Seasons and Principal Festivals of the Year* (Westminster, Md.: Carroll Press, 1950), I, p. 446. Cf. also *Sermones de Diversis*, 26, nos. 2f., PL 183:610 seq.

58. *Thesaurus Linguae Latinae*, V, I (Leipzig, 1909–1934), col. 1397–1399. Du Cange, *Glossarium* (Favre, 1884), III, p. 139.

59. Cf. R. Sprandel, *Ivo von Chartres und seine Stellung in der Kirchengeschichte* (Stuttgart, 1962), pp. 77–85: "Das Wesen der Dispensatio"; Bibliography,

then located at the beginning of an evolution of thought on the matter. When determining to what extent the abbot or the customs of a monastery could legitimately dispense one from the Rule of St Benedict, Bernard introduced certain distinctions. These rejected all that is contrary to what the Rule prescribes, as well as what is beside (*citra*) or beyond (*ultra*) the Rule, in order to maintain that which is in conformity with it (*secundum*).[60] Here we find a vocabulary which would become frequent and would be further enriched by the canonists of the second half of the twelfth century. They would speak of *dispensare cum*, or *contra*, or *praeter*, or *supra*, or *ultra*.[61]

Moreover this question of the limits within which one can dispense from the Rule is bound up with the exigencies of charity to the extent that there can be conflicts between the law, written or customary, and the love one owes to God and neighbor. In the course of the controversy between the Cluniacs and Cistercians, Peter the Venerable raised this delicate question.[62] The solution involved contributions from history, law and theology, some elements of which were still in the process of evolution at that time. The result was to be a very complex synthesis which would always

---

p. 77, no. 75. B. Jacqueline, "Yves de Chartres et St Bernard" in *Etudes d'Histoire du Droit Canonique Dédiées à Gabriel le Bras*, I (Paris, 1965), pp. 170–184, has established that St Bernard knew of Yvo's *Panormia*.

60. No. 11.

61. A number of texts of this type are cited by S. Kuttner, "Pope Lucius III and the Bigamous Archbishop of Palermo" in *Medieval Studies Presented to Aubrey Gwynn* SJ (Dublin, 1961), pp. 419–453. Later an abundant literature concerning dispensations (in the plural) began to appear, including for example the *Libellus de dispensationibus* of John of God which is cited, *ibid.*, p. 429, no. 87. Already in the second half of the twelfth century Richard of St Victor, in his *De questionibus Regule Sancti Augustini solutis* (ed. Marvin L. Colker, "Richard of Saint-Victor and the Anonymous of Bridlington" in *Traditio*, [1962]), when explaining the formula *secundum regulam* in relation to the profession of the Canons Regular according to the Rule of St Augustine, introduced this distinction: *quaedam in regula precipi, quaedam prohiberi, quaedam permitti.*

62. Cf. Peter the Venerable, *Letter* 111, *ed. cit.*, *passim*.

be in danger of losing its balance if any one of the elements were given too much emphasis. St Thomas, when formulating his synthesis, would incorporate into his doctrine on the moral obligation of religious Rules all that was essential in the teaching of St Bernard.[63]

Conclusion

Even when reduced to essentials St Bernard's teaching still seems speculative enough, not to say subtle. In any case, it is rigorously logical, following out to their conclusion a small number of principles. These had been laid down during the Carolingian renewal of the monastic ideal. St Bernard followed the tradition as it had been gradually developed since the ninth century, though he extended and enriched it. On more than one point the Cistercians had broken away from this tradition, going back beyond the accretions, multiplied through force of circumstances, to the basic observances of ancient monasticism and St Benedict's Rule.[64] But in regarding the Rule as the necessary and sufficient means by which monks achieve to purity of heart, they placed themselves within an evolutionary process to which St Benedict of Aniane and the ninth-century commentators on the Rule had given a definitive impetus.

We can but wonder at the constructive force with which St Bernard was able to weld these still rudimentary, half-expressed and scattered concepts into a tightly-woven synthesis. It is even more evident how conscious he was of practical necessities, and how he excelled in putting his ideas at the service of the monks of his day, to help them solve the concrete difficulties created by circumstances and particular situations.

Fundamentally, his teaching is based on the conviction that the Rule of St Benedict prescribes a manner of life, a *conversatio*, which,

---

63. *Summa Theologiae*, II–II, q. 186, a. 9. Mabillon summed up and praised this teaching of St Thomas in his Preface to this treatise (PL 182:859 ff).

64. Cf. P. Salmon, *op. cit.*

because it is a Christian way of life, necessarily means following and imitating Christ and so being incorporated into his Kingdom. It must therefore be evangelical, presenting the Gospel to monks in an institution to which they gain admittance by their profession, a second baptism. This should bring their first baptism to its fullest realization. Already sons of God, they now, under the impulse of grace, freely commit themselves to this life by a promise which entails the renunciation of the world and the total gift of themselves to God. They fulfill their vow by obeying the Rule, which is the Gospel expressed in terms relevant to their life.

This means in the concrete that the ascetical life is assigned a two-fold object—first, the moral precepts, which St Bernard calls "spiritual observances," everything relating to charity, humility, poverty, chastity and the other virtues, whose fulfillment is the most direct way of conforming to the saving will of God. Second, there are the "exterior observances," that is to say, those practices whose exercise promotes the fulfillment of the precepts; they include stability, silence, fasting, reading, work—in short, the discipline of the common life. St Bernard is convinced that St Benedict, under God's inspiration, knew instinctively how to ordain everything needful for the secure attainment of salvation, which is the one goal of all Christian and monastic life. Obeying the Rule is the most authentic way for monks of obeying God.

In practice this submission to God is expressed in submission to the abbot who, for the monk, is God's representative. But he too can only go to God by submitting to this Rule, the common norm of their obedience. In themselves the "exterior observances" are without doubt profitable means of fostering the practice of the evangelical virtues. However, they certainly do not all have an equal necessity. Their practical application may call for a certain amount of discernment, flexibility, even perhaps dispensation. So a monk needs a superior who will express for him in concrete terms the essential and universal obligations. Obeying the abbot will be his way then of obeying the Rule, and through the Rule, of obeying God. It is to this that he is bound by the profession promise made "according to the Rule," while the abbot, witnessing this pact between the monk and God, binds himself to insure its observance.

In this wonderfully consistent body of teaching, especially as it appears in the treatise, there is a harmonious blending of two aspects. These had been often propounded by other writers but always in isolation, when they ought actually to complement each other. They are, on the one hand, a theological view of the economy of salvation within the Church, and on the other, a juridical and practical concept of life in a monastic community, a life wholly ordered towards the union of man with God in Christ Jesus. St Bernard's synthesis corresponds perfectly with the structure, at once human and divine, of the Church itself, and with that mystery by which God communicates his own life to men in the Incarnation.

One can see then why this treatise has traditionally been considered an excellent commentary on the obedience taught by the Rule of St Benedict. Geoffrey of Auxerre called it a witness to the "discretion" of St Bernard.[65] The treatise was used towards the end of the twelfth century by the Premonstratension, Adam Scot,[66] but it was more widely circulated in the Benedictine and Cistercian monasteries. Fifty-seven manuscripts of the twelfth or early thirteenth century come to us from this source.[67] Later it was especially among the Benedictines that De Precepto was considered as a commentary on the Rule of St Benedict and transcribed with it.[68]

---

65. Vita prima S. Bernardi, III, 29: Si vigil in eodem zelo et circumspecta (quaeritur) discretio, De precepto et dispensatione disserens audiatur (PL 185:320).

66. De ordine, professione et habitu canonicorum Ordinis Praemonstratensis, Sermon 7, nos. 4–6, PL 198:499–501. It is inspired by nos. 44–46 of this treatise.

67. A list of these manuscripts can be found in S. Bernardi Opera, III (Rome: Editiones Cistercienses, 1963), pp. 244–247.

68. This is brought out by the manuscripts which have been cited in the article, "S. Bernard commentateur de S. Benoît, Etudes sur S. Bernard et le texte de ses Ecrits" in Analecta Sacri Ordinis Cisterciensis, 9 (1953), pp. 148–150. Additional citations will be found in Recueil, II, pp. 44–48. In a manuscript of Arras (no. 706, twelfth or thirteenth century from Saint Vaast, a Benedictine monastery) the third book of Rupert of Deutz's Commentary on the Rule of St Benedict (PL 170:511–526) has been inserted into the text of Bernard's treatise.

Later Mabillon rendered eloquent homage to the value of this
treatise for monks.[69]

One of the texts to which St Bernard refers when he is speaking
of the obligation created by the vows is this verse of Psalm sixty-
five: *Reddam tibi vota mea quae distinxerunt labia mea*—I will render
unto you the vows which my lips have uttered.[70] In using it he
alludes to a vast store of traditional doctrine. Later it was given a
much greater importance than that given to it by Bernard. Sometimes it was even presented as the biblical foundation for the vows
of the religious life. One can see what difficulties such a theory

69. "Among those who follow the monastic way of life, it is evident that
the more dedicated one becomes, the more he will be concerned with the
spirit of the Rule rather than with its obligations, and the more he will seek
to plumb the mind of the legislator rather than the opinions of the casuists.
When he is devoted to his Rule with his whole heart, and has become perfectly
subject to it, he will have nothing more at heart than to follow its guidance in
all things, even if there be no obligation. For religious such as these there is no
law, and they may perhaps have less need of reading this treatise than those
who are always carefully examining the exact extent of the obligations of each
rule rather than troubling about its truest interpretation and best practice.
These latter consult the authors in order to minimize the onus of the Rule and,
as much as they may without sin, to draw back from a conscientious (or as
they call it, over-scrupulous) observance thereof. The worst thing that can
happen to these religious is for them to fall in with teachers willing to pander
to their weakness, who actually advise them to follow the line of least
resistance. This can gradually lead, first to neglect, then to contempt, and
finally to hatred of the Rule, to the grave peril of their souls.

In my opinion they could hardly find a better and safer doctor to instruct
them than Bernard, since he is endowed with all those qualities which most
commend a religious guide: namely, an uncommon piety, an inspired doctrine, and a most thorough familiarity with things monastic. Consequently,
his opinions on these matters can hardly be called into question, but rather
are altogether true, straight from the heart, and to be embraced by all classes
of Benedictines.

I would even venture to say that were we permitted to summon the saint
of our choice to return to earth and instruct us in these matters, we could do
no better than to choose to listen to Bernard. We ought, certainly, to be
grateful to the monks of Saint Peter's of Chartres for obtaining the holy
abbot's opinions and doctrine on this subject. It would be interesting to know
about the details of their petition and the circumstances of its satisfaction"
(PL 182:8 57ff.).

70. Ps 65:13–14 (Vulgate).

could and did cause for a man like Luther. He criticized the vows
as being contrary to the Word of God, to faith, to evangelical
liberty, to the commandments of God, and to reason itself. Certainly this can be understood as opposition to certain historical
expressions of the religious life. But "the problems raised by Luther
regarding monastic life were insoluble given the theological pre-
suppositions of the sixteenth century. Given the perspectives of
today, especially those of the Second Vatican Council, in regard to
the Church and the religious life, they are no longer insoluble."[71]
They are in fact already solved in many of the reformed Churches
by the very existence within them of religious who do make vows.[72]
One can even say that the problem no longer exists—it has no
object. The carefully nuanced doctrine of St Bernard concerning
the voluntary character of the obligations undertaken at profession,
their compatibility with spiritual liberty, and the limits of a Rule
in regard to material observances, enables us to place the vows in
their true perspective. It is this true perspective which Protestant
religious share today with their brethren in the Catholic Church.

Clervaux Abbey,   Jean Leclercq OSB
      Luxembourg

EDITOR'S NOTE

The translation of St Bernard's *Book on Precept and Dispensation*
presented here is based on the critical Latin text prepared by Jean
Leclercq OSB and Henri Rochais OSB and published in the third
volume of *S. Bernardi Opera*. This text is basically that of the Dijon
manuscript 658 which comes from the Library of Cîteaux. The
manuscript was probably copied within ten years of the death of

71. Otto Pesch, "Luthers Kritik am Mönchtum in katholischer Sicht' 'in
Strukturen christlicher Existenz, Festgabe F. Wulf (Würzburg, 1967), pp. 81-96.
72. Cf. P. Anson, *The Call of the Cloister* (London: SPCK, 1955); J. Heijke,
An Ecumenical Light on the Renewal of Religious Community Life: Taizé
(Pittsburgh: Duquesne University Press, 1967).

St Bernard, perhaps even while he was still alive. We have incorporated into the text, as did the critical edition, the subtitles drawn from the Lilienfeld manuscript 96. Although these are of the thirteenth century they are inspired by earlier titles. They are more sober than later collections, come from a Cistercian source and help to evoke the monastic milieu for which this treatise was written and in which it was read, copied and interpreted.

The Scripture passages have been translated to fit the context. While the references follow the Revised Standard Version it must be remembered that St Bernard was familiar with the Vulgate which differs in part from this English version. Where Bernard has drawn from the Septuagint or some version other than the Vulgate this has been noted.

INTRODUCTORY LETTER

TO THE LORD ABBOT OF COULOMBS,[1] abiding health in the Lord from brother Bernard, who is called Abbot of Clairvaux.

I am now sending you as I promised my answer to the letters of the two monks of Chartres.[2] Although I had at first intended to be brief and respond with a mere letter, I have complied with your wishes in writing at some length.[3] As you can see for yourself, I have yielded to your persuasion and made a book of it, so that many people may be edified by many words.

When you have read this work, send it to the abbot rather than to the monks of Chartres. They may see it later, if he thinks fit. After all, they are monks, and according to their Rule they may not send or receive letters without their superior's consent.[4] Indeed as you know, it is on this account that I have delayed my reply in spite of their importunity, because I suspected they had presumed to write to me without their abbot's knowledge. I was not mistaken, as I have learned since.

1. This was Roger who was abbot of Coulombs from 1119 to 1173 or 1174.
2. The precise identity of these two monks remains unknown. They were undoubtedly monks of the Benedictine abbey of Saint-Père-en-Vallée, near Chartres.
3. Cf. *infra*, no. 61.
4. Cf. *St Benedict's Rule for Monasteries* (hereafter RB), 54:1. (For citations of RB we will use the division of chapter and verse of E. Manning [Westmalle, 1962], who follows Lentini-Hanslik.)

103

H

As the reader may see for himself, I began my work under the form of a letter, but since in complying with your request I have exceeded that measure, it had rather be called a book. Among the many difficulties which I have there unraveled, those dealing with precepts which may be dispensed, by whom, and to what measure, are the more involved and the more important. Let it therefore be called, *On Precept and Dispensation*, unless you are able to think of something more appropriate.

ON PRECEPT AND DISPENSATION

I CAN DEFER no longer, yet dare I speak? You have compelled me by your frequent letters and messages either to betray my ineptitude or to fail in charity, and I would rather be found lacking in that which "puffs up" than deficient in that which "edifies."[5] So I yield now to your entreaties and take these difficult knots into my hands. I fear these hands shall be wounded before we are done, but it is vain for me to plead. It seems that my own spoken and written words have led me into this. How can I maintain my incompetence when you insist that my own expressed ideas prove the contrary? It is on this faith of yours then rather than on any faith in myself that I now enter the deep. God knows how I will ever get out! If only your powers of judgment were equal to your charity! If the results fall short of expectation, lay it rather to your error in estimating my abilities than to any lack of good will on my part.

I shall try to treat these questions briefly in the form of a letter but I fear the letter itself will be far from brief. I can hardly solve these matters in less space than you took to state them, and you consumed two fairly long letters in doing only that.

I. 1. The first question then, deals with our Rule, and if I am not mistaken, all or nearly all the others stem from this. You ask how

5. Cf. 1 Cor 8:1.

seriously a monastic rule is to be taken by those who profess it, and whether all its precepts are to be considered as binding under pain of sin. Are they commands, or only counsels or admonitions that may be lightly promised and lightly transgressed? Are some counsels and others commands, so that we may ignore the former so long as we keep the latter? If this last question be answered in the affirmative, I am to distinguish for you which are which, lest each follow his own particular ideas and thus perhaps strain out the gnats and swallow the camels,[6] not knowing how much care and effort to bestow on each observance.

Such is as far as I can recall the substance of your main question, if not your exact words. As for your other question on the nature of obedience, its degrees and limits, I believe it is so bound up with this first one on the nature of the Rule that in answering the first the second will also become clear.

The obligation of a Rule for those who have professed it

2. As I see it then, the Rule of St Benedict is proposed to all, but imposed on none. It will be of profit to those who reverently receive it and keep it, but no obstacle to those who pass it by. That which depends on the free will of him who undertakes it rather than on the authority of him who proposes it, I would definitely consider as a free offering and not as a matter of duty. However, if a man has once made this free-will offering and promised to be faithful to it in the future, he is henceforth obliged to what he was formerly free to refuse. One is no longer free, but obliged to honor one's promise. He is bound to keep the vows his own lips have pronounced,[7] and from his own mouth he will be condemned or justified.[8] As a certain saint tells us, this is a happy necessity which forces us to improve ourselves.[9]

---

6. Cf. Mt 23:24.   7. Cf. Ps 66:13f.; Deut 23:23.

8. Cf. Job 9:20; Lk 19:22; Mt 12:37.

9. St Augustine, *Letter* 127, 8 (CSEL 44:28): *Felix et necessitas, quae in meliora compellet*; trans. Sr W. Parsons SND, *St Augustine's Letters* (New York: Fathers of the Church, 1953), vol. I, p. 356.

The prescriptions of the Rule: commands or counsels

This holds good for all the prescriptions of the Rule except those spiritual precepts of divine institution which St Benedict merely repeats, such as admonitions to the practice of charity, humility, meekness. These can hardly be called into question. As for the rest, they are to be considered as counsels and admonitions, which may be passed over without fault, for those who have not promised to observe them, but as precepts, binding under sin, for those who have so promised. To use your own terms, it is a matter of free choice for the former, but a necessity and even a sort of natural exigency for the latter. However, this necessity is such as to admit of certain necessary and reasonable dispensations.

II. 3. The power of dispensing in these matters is not entrusted to all, but only to those who can say with the Apostle, "Let a man so account us as servants of Christ and dispensers of the mysteries fo God."[10] The good and faithful servant whom the Lord has set over his household[11] knows that he should incur expense only when he may thus gain some recompense for his master. "Now this is required of dispensers, that the man be found trustworthy."[12] May not the same degree of trustworthiness be demanded of the subject who avails himself of the dispensation as of the superior who gives it?

From what has been said thus far, you may gather that your distinctions are valid, so long as the proper allowances are made for circumstances. As regards the subject, the precepts of the Rule (in external matters at least) are voluntary at first, but necessary once he has promised to observe them. From the superior's point of view, they are voluntary if of human institution and necessary if of divine institution.

---

10. I Cor 4:1f.   11. Cf. Mt 24:45; Lk 12:42.
12. I Cor 4:2.

Stable, firm, and fixed necessity

4. Perhaps all this will be more clearly and easily seen if necessity is divided into three degrees: first the *stable*, second the *firm*, and third the *fixed*.[13]

Stable necessity

I would call that sort of necessity *stable* which can only be changed by the "dispensers of the mysteries of God" [14] that is, by the superiors of the various regular institutes such as the Basilians, Augustinians, Benedictines, Canons Regular, and any other institutes of legitimate authority. These Rules have been handed down to us by saints and holy men and are to be kept inviolable by their subjects, who should never be permitted to change them in any way. However, since they were established by men, they may be lawfully and safely dispensed from according to circumstances, time, place, and persons, by those men who have inherited this authority through legitimate elections. Let the reader note that I have not said that they can be changed at will for light reasons by such authority, but only dispensed from carefully and reasonably. They can be so changed by these men because they are not of their very nature or in themselves good, but only contingently good.

5. These rules were devised or ordained, not because it is unlawful to live in a different manner, but because this manner of life was found to be expedient for the gaining or the preservation of charity. So long as they serve this end, they stand fixed and immutable and cannot licitly be changed, even by superiors. However, should they ever be found contrary to charity by those to whom God has granted insight and entrusted with authority, is it not clearly just and fitting that they should be omitted, interrupted, or altered for

13. *Stabilis, inviolabilis, incommutabilis.*
14. Cf. 1 Cor 1:4.

the sake of the very charity which conceived them? It would certainly be blameworthy to hold in opposition to charity that which was ordained solely for charity. So then let those prescriptions which we have classified as of stable necessity be respected even by superiors, so long as they serve the interests of charity.

Am I the only one to hold this view or the first to have stated it? Did not Pope Gelasius think the same? It was he who said, "Except in cases of necessity, the ordinances of the saintly Fathers are to remain inviolate."[15] And Pope Leo also, "Except in cases of necessity, the ordinances of the saintly Fathers are not to be violated in any way." He further says, "Where there is true necessity, those who have the power to dispense are to use it for the good of the Church. Changes in law must be based on necessity."[16]

Firm necessity

III. 6. By what I have called *firm* necessity I understand those laws which are not of man, but of God, and which can only be changed by him who made them. Such are for example, "You shall not kill; you shall not commit adultery; you shall not steal,"[17] and those others engraved on the tables of the Law. Although they may not be dispensed from by any human power, nor was nor will ever any man be allowed to set them aside,[18] the Lord himself sets aside those he chooses when he chooses; as when the Egyptians were despoiled by the Hebrews,[19] or as when the Prophet was commanded to make love to a prostitute.[20] What else would these be but serious sins of theft and fornication, were not both excused by

---

15. Cf. St Gelasius I, *Letter* 9, ch. 24 (PL 59:55b). Here and in the following quotation from Pope Leo, St Bernard uses the text found in Ivo of Chartres (PL 161:57a), but Ivo was only paraphrasing the pontiffs, though he did this accurately enough.

16. Cf. St Leo I, *Letter* 167 (PL 54:1202); trans. C. L. Feltoe, *The Letters and Sermons of Leo the Great, Bishop of Rome* (*Nicene and Post-Nicene Fathers*, second series, New York: Christian Literature, 1895), vol. 12, pp. 109ff.

17. Ex 20:13ff.   18. Cf. Mt 5:19.
19. Cf. Ex 3:22.   20. Cf. Hos 1:2.

the authority of him who commanded them? Whenever we read of similar actions performed by holy men without any evidence of a command from God, we must assume either that they sinned (for they were men) or that they had received some divine revelation (for they were men of God). For example there is the case of Samson, who killed himself as well as his foes.[21] If we choose to defend his action we must suppose he had received some revelation, although scripture does not affirm this.

Fixed necessity

7. But what is to be understood by the third kind of necessity, which I have called *fixed* necessity? Fittingly enough it may be referred to that necessity so fixed by God from eternity that it can in no way be altered even by God himself. Under this heading falls that spiritual doctrine and teaching on charity, humility, meekness, and the other virtues, which we find set forth in both the Old and New Testaments, but especially in the Sermon on the Mount. These virtues are so precious that it is never expedient or lawful to be without them. They stand fixed because they are good in their very nature and can never be commanded or observed except as good and tending towards good. At all times and for all persons they bring salvation when they are kept and cause death when they are rejected.

The first sort of necessity then is founded on the free will of the subject, the second on the authority of the commanding power, and the third on the excellence of the thing commanded.

8. As we have said already, these three necessities differ as to their degree of immutability. The first, while not wholly immutable, can hardly be said to be changeable, for it may only be changed by proper authority and by a responsible and prudent dispensation. The second is almost unchangeable, and is greater, because it can be changed by God alone as we have seen. The third and greatest

21. Cf. Judg 16:30.

is entirely changeless, because even God is not free to alter it. Thus we may call the first which no man can change except superiors, "hardly-changeable" necessity, the second which God alone can change, "almost-unchangeable" necessity, and the third which even he cannot change "entirely-changeless" necessity.

IV. 9. Now that we have disposed of that, we may return to our main question. It should be clear that the greater part of our rules are subject, if not to the free will, at any rate to the discretion of the superior. "But," you may object, "what is left then of the necessity which you are referring to?" A great deal, I say; let me explain.

The abbot is not above the Rule—for he himself has professed it

In the first place, as we have already seen, the spiritual precepts of the Rule are not in the hands of the abbot. The other prescriptions dealing with outward observances are not subject to his will either to the extent that it becomes their norm. Charity rather is to be the norm. Nor is the abbot above the Rule,[22] for he himself once freely placed himself beneath it. There is only one power above the Rule of St Benedict which we must admit, and that is God's Rule, charity. Let the letter of the Rule give way then, for a time, to charity when need arises, but God forbid that it ever bow to any mere man's will. He who has been chosen abbot is placed as judge, not over the traditions of the Fathers, but over the transgressions of his brethren, that he may uphold the rules and punish offences. Indeed, I consider that those holy observances are rather entrusted to the prudence and faithfulness of the superiors than subjected to their will. Thus our holy Legislator, in leaving anything to the abbot's choice, was careful (as far as I can recall) not to use the term "will." He rather used such expressions as consideration,[23] disposition,[24] providence,[25]

22. RB 41:4; 55:8.
23. Consideration: RB 34:2; 53:19; 55:3.
24. Disposition: RB 3:6; 41:5; 63:2; 65:12.
25. Providence: RB 41:4; 55:8.

or judgment [26] since he wished the good and faithful steward to dispense according to objective reason rather than according to his own will. Hence he reminds him more than once of the account he will one day have to give God concerning these matters.[27]

10. I read in the Rule, "These things are for the abbot to consider,"[28] and this or that is left to the discretion, judgment, or disposition of the abbot;[29] but I remember reading nothing about his changing things at his pleasure. On the contrary we read, "Let all follow the Rule as their guide, and let no one rashly depart from it"[30]—no one, including the abbot. "Let all follow the Rule," he says, because "no one is to follow his own will."[31] This too, I believe, includes the abbot. Do you not see that he has his obligations too, and is not so free as you might think? In addition does not the very act of profession in which the subject submits himself to the superior also bind the superior? I consider it a bi-lateral contract which binds both parties, the promise of the one places them mutually in debt; the one owes faithful solicitude, the other, humble obedience. What room here for freedom, when the superior himself has assumed an obligation? The freedom of the superior is further circumscribed in that the subject promises not unqualified obedience, but specifically obedience according to a Rule, and to no other Rule than that of St Benedict. Therefore he who governs should not lay the reins of his own will over the backs of his subjects, but acknowledge the limits set for him in the Rule. He is to confine his commands to what he has determined to be the right path; not just any right path, but the one pointed out by the same blessed Father, or at any rate, one which is in conformity with his spirit. Thus runs the formula of profession: "I promise," not the Rule, but, "obedience according to the Rule of St Benedict." "According to the Rule," and therefore not according to the will of the superior. If, once I have made such a profession, my abbot attempts to impose upon me something which is not according to

26. Judgment: RB 3:5; 39:6; 40:5; 65:11.
27. RB 2:34, 37f.; 3:11; 63:3; 65:22.
28. RB 53:3.   29. Cf. *supra*, notes 23–26.   30. RB 3:7.
31. RB 3:8.

the Benedictine Rule, and which is also not in accord with the Rules of St Basil, Augustine, or Pachomius, to what obligation, I ask, have I to conform? I can be obliged to perform only that which I have promised.

The limits of obedience

V. 11. Now you can see the extent of your obligation to obey, which you asked me to define. If the measure of obedience be the tenor of the profession, the power of command can hardly extend farther. Obedience then is limited to what is neither beside, beyond, nor contrary to the same tenor of profession. Therefore, anyone having made profession in any form of religious life is not to be driven beyond nor restrained short of that which he has professed. Even less can he be obliged to anything contrary to the same profession. Hence this central norm of life established by vow and reinforced by public profession, is likened to the tree of life in the midst of Paradise;[32] the only law which the subject can be obliged to obey. Let not the commands or prohibitions of the superior over-step these bounds. They cannot be stretched farther nor cut shorter. Let no superior forbid me to fulfill my promises, nor demand more. My vows cannot be added to without my concurrence, nor diminished without clear necessity. True necessity knows no law and hence justifies dispensations; however free will, which alone can deserve punishment, is also our only means of progress. On the one hand, when we have used this free will to make a vow and then fail to fulfill it, without the necessity which justifies a dispensation, we are guilty, dispensation or not. On the other hand, if our will be constrained we gain no merit, but rather incur the guilt of murmurers. Let superiors then hold their subjects to what these themselves have promised rather than to their own whims, and let them urge rather than force them to better things. Let them condescend to dispense when there is reasonable need, but let them never be party to mere backsliding.

32. Cf. Gen 2:9.

Perfect obedience

VI. 12. For the rest, let the subject know that this sort of obedience which is confined to the limits of the vows is quite imperfect. Perfect obedience knows no law. It can be held within no limits. Not content with the narrow bounds of obligation, it spreads to the fullness of charity, carried by its generous will. Eager for every order in the strength of its free and ready spirit, it considers not the measure, but reaches out in boundless liberty. It is this which the apostle Peter described when he wrote, "Purifying your hearts by the obedience of charity,"[33] thus aptly distinguishing this sort of obedience from that other dead and servile sort which is not moved by love, but compelled by fear. This obedience is proper to the just man for whom there is no law;[34] not that he lives outside the law, but neither is he under it. Indeed he is not at all content with the mere obligations of his profession, but goes beyond them in his dedication. The Rule itself is not silent on this, but mentions it in discussing how a brother should behave when given impossible commands. He is counseled to, "Confide in God's help and obey out of love;"[35] and again the third step of humility is, "that a monk submit himself to his superior in all obedience."[36] It says "all," wishing us not to rest content with the mere tenor of our profession, not to wait until we are obliged nor to limit ourselves to agreed terms, but gladly go beyond our vows and obey in all.

As regards time, the limits of obedience are extended to the very limits of time, so that we must obey as long as we live. The Only-begotten Son of God has here set us the supreme example, for he obeyed his Father even unto death.[37] To stop short of that would be disobedience, unfaithfulness, transgression and sin.

All disobedience is not equally serious

VII. 13. It will be worthwhile to examine the causes, motives, and intentions of disobedience; also to determine which commands

33. 1 Pet 1:22.   34. Cf. 1 Tim 1:9.   35. RB 68:5.
36. RB 7:34.   37. Cf. Phil 2:8.

may occasion it, and from whom. I deem that no act of disobedience whatever is to be taken lightly, although there are degrees of this evil. For instance, God has commanded, "You shall not kill."[38] Suppose we have two murderers, the one acting out of a desire for plunder and the other in self-defense. Is there not a vast degree of difference in the guilt of these two "lepers,"[39] though their ill deeds are alike? Let us further suppose the one to have given way to sudden anger, and the other to have plotted his act with deliberate and deep-rooted malice. Are they to be judged alike in spite of the disparity of motive? Again, on the face of it, what could be more wicked than the incestuous trickery of the daughters of Lot?[40] Yet who can fail to see that their guilt was diminished if not blotted out by the piety of their intent and the intent of their piety?

The different authorities and precepts

Now as regards the matter of a precept and the dignity of him who gives it, we must recognize certain distinctions. The greater reverence due the authority of the superior, the more we should fear offending him, and the greater will be the guilt of the transgression; likewise the gravity of the matter involved can augment one's guilt. Thus it is better to obey God than man;[41] among men, better to obey superiors than equals,[42] and better to obey our own superiors than someone else's. If it is better to obey these, it is also worse to disobey them.

14. It is much the same as to the matter; the weightier matter requiring more, and the lighter less care and diligence in execution. Contempt of these is also more or less serious in proportion to the obligation. I consider those commands grave or light which are so

38. Ex 20:13.

39. Cf. Deut 17:8. Bernard is here alluding to the Vulgate text which speaks of distinguishing "between leper and leper." The literal meaning of the Hebrew *negah* is scourge. Since leprosy is the "scourge" par excellence, the Vulgate so translated it.

40. Cf. Gen 19:30ff.   41. Cf. Acts 5:29.   42. Cf. RB 71:3.

according to the will of the authority in question, be it God or man. For instance, we are commanded, "You shall not steal,"[43] and again, "Give to all who ask you."[44] Both commands are from God himself, and both are important, but that concerning theft is more binding. Everyone knows that God is most just, and is not equally displeased by theft and mere stinginess; that he prefers us to keep what is ours rather than to take what is another's. Consequently miserliness is a lesser fault than larceny.

15. Likewise with the commands of men—they are seldom of equal weight, since the will of those who command is more or less moved according to needs and circumstances. That which they consider more right and fitting, they will the more desire and require to be done. Therefore, the gravity of the precept depends primarily on the authority of him who issues it; the reward of obedience and the burden of disobedience following here the same measure. When, as we have seen, a higher superior commands in a weightier matter, a more careful obedience is in order and a greater guilt may be incurred by contempt.

16. When we have grasped these distinctions we will be able to determine easily the measure of our obedience and the weight of our disobedience. We can now not only tell day from night,[45] that is, the good of obedience from the evil of disobedience, but also day from day and night from night; or to put it more clearly, good from better and bad from worse.

The degrees of obedience

Obedience is "good," according to our Father St Benedict, when one obeys out of fear of hell, or out of faithfulness to one's vows;[46] it is better when one obeys out of love of God, substituting charity for necessity; and it is perfect, in my opinion, when the command is received in the spirit in which it is given. When the will of the

43. Rom 13:9.   44. Lk 6:30.   45. Cf. Jer 33:25.
46. RB 5:3.

subject is conformed to that of the superior, the subject, in carrying out his orders, will not be likely to confuse greater matters with lesser or lesser with greater (as often happens). With a tranquil mind he will match his care to the weight of the matter in hand, both in fulfilling what is commanded, and in avoiding what is prohibited. Not that the least command is to be despised, but only that it be recognized for what it is, the least: the least that is in comparison with what is greater. The obedient man who is both faithful and humble knows how to bestow fitting care on what is more important without neglecting what is less so, recognizing by the sure instinct of a devoted heart which commands are to be obeyed in what manner, saying with the prophet, "You have commanded your precepts to be most carefully observed."[47] Since he does not say, "all your precepts," those only are to be understood which, because the transgression necessarily involves a serious fault, cannot be transgressed without incurring a serious penalty, as for example, "You shall not kill"[48] and the like. Obedience to such commands is never unjust or evil, and they can never be licitly set aside, at least not by any mere human power.

VIII. 17. The others which may be dispensed from by the proper authorities, and which are enforced by lighter sanctions, may be considered as lighter. I mean, for example, the prescriptions regarding conversation and laughter. These things are licit when there is no rule against them. When there is such a rule it is sinful to break it, but not gravely so especially if the fault be palliated by surprise or forgetfulness.

Contempt would be another matter. These precepts which you have termed "optional" were devised by way of means and are quite different from those necessarily imposed by the nature of things; however they cannot be neglected without fault nor despised without sin, because they are commanded by those to whom it is said, "He who hears you hears me, and he who despises you despises me."[49] The thing in itself may be harmless, but when

47. Ps 119:4.   48. Ex 20:13.   49. Lk 10:16.

authority has forbidden it, it becomes binding under pain of sin. However, the sin would not be serious except in cases of contempt.

18. This you may take as a general rule for all those things which are neither good nor bad in themselves or in their inseparable consequences, and which are not fixed by divine law or by one's holy profession: they may be either done or omitted licitly so long as there is no ruling on the subject, but once there is a ruling it may not be neglected without fault nor despised without sin. Neglect is always culpable and contempt is always damnable. They differ; neglect arises from laziness, but contempt from swollen pride.

Contempt is always equally serious

Contempt is always serious, whatever the importance or triviality of the matter, and it is usually a grave sin. The gravity of the sin of neglect, however, varies according to that of the command in question. We may liken contempt to adultery, which is always a serious sin, whatever the circumstances or intent. But a light word which slips out in a time or place of silence, or uncontrolled laughter which is more a reflex than a reasoned act, although they may be symptoms of a careless or dissipated soul, are none the less easily forgiven, since they are faults rather than sins. But what if one were to give rein to idle words deliberately and knowingly? Even if he had permission to speak, would he not be breaking the Rule of Truth himself and would he not be called to account for it on the day of judgment? The Judge himself has warned us of those idle words for every one of which he will then demand an account.[50] Woe unto us! How shall we be able to justify our idleness? But if a word is uttered for some particular reason it can no longer be classified as idle. Indeed, who does not know how a single word of detraction can outweigh innumerable idle words in guilt and punishment? Why so? Simply because they fall under laws of varying gravity and, as we have seen, the transgression of the weightier law is greater, just as that of the lighter law is lesser.

50. Cf. Mt 12:36.

Subjects should not obey commands which are contrary to God

IX. 19. It is not quite the same as regards the person who gives the command, for whether it be God himself or some man who holds his place, one should comply with the same care and reverence to all commands, unless the one be found contrary to the other. In that case, I would counsel imitation of the apostle Peter who said, "We must obey God rather than men."[51] We must answer thus with the apostles lest we hear with the pharisees, "Why have you also transgressed the command of God for the sake of your traditions?"[52] But if we are grieved when we must so offend a human master out of faithfulness to the divine Master, we may console ourselves with the saying of holy Samuel which you yourselves quoted, in which he distinguishes between two evils[53] thus: "If a man offend his fellow, he may yet seek mercy from God; but if he sin against God, who will plead for him?"[54] If I were to find myself in such a dilemma that I must offend God or man I would freely choose the safer and more just course of not offending God. I have in this saying of the Prophet my consolation: the mercy of God. If I were to choose the other alternative and offend God, who would plead for me? Were I to turn to any man, I would incur the reproach of scripture which says, "Cursed be he who places his trust in man,"[55] and I would deserve it. If one sins against God, even for the sake of some man, who indeed is to plead for him? Alas, no one! The prayer of the one who caused the offence is no more acceptable to God than that of the offender. We have need of an advocate who is on good terms with the offended party.

The fault, if it be a fault, committed against the man who is so disobeyed is attenuated, if not cancelled out, by the higher good in view. Consequently, when we read: "If a man offend his fellow,"[56] we should add, "for God's sake," since otherwise one would also be

---

51. Acts 5:29.   52. Mt 15:3.
53. Lit. "between leper and leper." Cf. note 39, *supra.*
54. 1 Kings 2:25.   55. Jer 17:5.   56. 1 Kings 2:25.

I

offending God. No other motive can excuse one from fault in such a case, particularly if the fellow man in question be a superior. Otherwise the Prophet would be contradicting that saying of St Paul: "Sinning thus against your brother you sin against Christ."[57] And again Truth himself has said to superiors: "He who despises you despises me."[58] But all our fellow men are included according to that other text: "See that you despise not any of these little ones[59] . . . he who scandalizes one of these little ones. . . ."[60] May God spare us, my brothers, for you know the rest!

Scandal

20. But not all scandals are to be weighed in the same balance. Very different from that of the little ones is the scandal of the pharisees. When the fearful apostles foresaw that these latter would be scandalized by the words of Truth, they were told, "Leave them alone, they are blind and leaders of the blind."[61] The first sort of scandal comes from ignorance, whereas the second is the fruit of malice. The one is scandalized because it knows not truth, the other because it hates truth. I believe this is why the former are called "little ones." They have good will, but lack wisdom; they have the zeal of God, but not according to knowledge.[62] Such scandals are apt to inspire solicitude rather than wrath, at least in the hearts of spiritual men. Thus St Paul teaches us: "You who are spiritual, instruct such a one in all meekness."[63] It would be most ungracious for a mere man to be angry with those to whom God has shown so much understanding, for the very executioners of the Lord were not excluded from his compassion. They were great sinners, but poor judges, and as deserving of compassion for the blindness of their judgment as of wrath for the greatness of their sin. They would have been blessed had they not been scandalized at him, according to his own words,[64] but now they are only miserable, so do not refuse

57. 1 Cor 8:12.   58. Lk 10:16.   59. Mt 18:12.
60. Mk 9:41.   61. Mt 15:14   62. Cf. Rom. 10:2.
63. Gal 6:1.   64. Cf. Mt 11:6.

them commiseration. Even in the midst of his passion the Lord was moved to compassion and lovingly prayed from his cross: "Father, forgive them," and as if casting about for some palliative to their horrible crime, added, "for they know not what they do."[65] As if to say: "They are worthy of pardon, because they are little ones in understanding. I know not their guilt, for they knew not my Godhead. Indeed, had they known, they would never have crucified the Lord of Glory.[66] But I recognize the guilt of those others, who have recognized and hated both me and my Father."[67]

St Paul too, fearing for the ignorance of such "little ones," reproached the wisdom of him who did not know how to condescend to their weakness: "Shall that weak brother perish on account of this knowledge of yours; he for whom Christ has died?"[68]

The precepts of superiors to be obeyed as the commands of God

21. If we must be so careful then not to offend the "little ones," how much more careful ought we to be about offending religious superiors? God has, after a fashion, put them on an equal footing with himself. He has even imputed to himself the respect as well as the contempt shown to them, for he explicitly told them, "He who hears you hears me; and he who despises you despises me."[69] Do we not find the same thought in our holy Rule where it says, "The obedience which is offered to superiors is shown to God?"[70]

Therefore, whatever such a man commands in God's name, if it be not clearly displeasing to God, is to be taken as if commanded by God himself. What difference does it make if God speaks in person or if he speaks through his ministers, be these angels or men? "But," you may protest, "men are often mistaken in their apprehension of what is God's will in cases of doubt, and so may lead us astray." And what is that to you, who are more ignorant than they are? Don't you remember that passage of Scripture which says,

65. Lk 23:34. 66. 1 Cor 2:8. 67. Jn 15:24.
68. 1 Cor 8:11. 69. Lk 10:16. 70. RB 5:15.

"The lips of the priest shall keep wisdom, and the law shall be sought from his mouth, for he is the angel of the Lord of hosts?"[71]

We are to seek the law from his mouth, but I do not believe this means that he has to tell us what we can learn for ourselves from Scripture and right reason; in such matters his commands or prohibitions would be superfluous or invalid. Rather it means that the wise lips of the angel of the Lord are to reveal God's will to us in doubtful cases, when there is no other means at hand for learning it. From whom could we better seek insight into God's designs than from him who has been established as a dispenser of the mysteries of God?[72] Let us then accept as from God himself all the words of him who is God's representative, so long as he does not speak against God.

22. We are not now contradicting the holy prophet Samuel, when we admit men to possess divine authority to this extent. There is certainly a difference between the two types of authority, as was demonstrated above concerning this same text from the prophet.[73] It is rather that what we have admitted in cases of doubt he denies in cases where there is no doubt, so that, as we have seen, the words "for God's sake" ought to be understood as added to the proposition "if a man offend his fellow." Unfortunately, men often do abuse their authority to the extent of presuming to countermand the clear ordinances of God.

It is this which has furnished you with the occasion as well as with the subject matter of your argument, for you assert that this imputing of divine authority to the commands and ordinances of men makes it difficult, if not impossible, for the subject to save his soul. In support of this you adduce the vast number of imperious commands which superiors are wont to heap carelessly upon the backs of their subjects and which are very difficult, if not entirely impossible to observe.

X.   23. I do not deny that the perfection of obedience is a difficult undertaking, but only for those who attempt it with the wrong

71. Mal 2:7.   72. 1 Cor 4:1.   73 Cf. 1 Kings 2:25. See also n. 19 above.

dispositions. After all, it is a sign of an imperfect heart and a perverted will to examine cautiously the injunctions of our seniors; to hesitate at each command; to demand to know the reason for everything; to suspect the worst if this be denied us; never to obey willingly unless we are commanded something that suits us, or which has been demonstrated to our satisfaction as necessary or useful. Obedience such as this is indeed a touchy affair and certainly a heavy burden as well, but this is not the obedience described in our Rule: "Obedience without delay."[74] This is to examine in the cunning of one's heart rather than to obey "at the hearing of the ear."[75] It is no wonder that worldly souls are not only weighed down, but actually overwhelmed by this rashly assumed burden; for weak human nature simply cannot bear what is intended only for generous spirits.[76] To such it is a light burden and a sweet yoke, because it is the burden and the yoke of Christ.[77] But to those who have not the Spirit of Christ it remains utterly insupportable. If you were referring to such as these, you were right in saying that the Rule is a "law" which has "entered in that sin might abound."[78] This is not the fault of the law or of the lawgiver, but of those who rashly undertake what they are unwilling to observe. "The law indeed is holy and just," but since you knew yourself to be a worldly-minded person, "sold under sin,"[79] why did you not take thought beforehand? This is a Gospel tower whose foundations should not be laid until the builder has sat down and taken stock of his resources. You have no choice now except to accept correction and obey those placed over you, or to bear in shame the taunt: "This man undertook to build, and was not able to finish."[80]

24. But perhaps you will say: "Can anyone whomsoever be found who has attained such perfection that he will not slip up on some one of the numberless picayune regulations which superiors are wont to strew about so carelessly?" I can hardly pretend to be able to produce such a one when the Apostles themselves confess: "We all offend in many things;"[81] and, "If we say we have no sin,

---

74. RB 5:1. 75. Ps 18:44; RB 5:5. 76. Cf. Mt 26:41.
77. Cf. Mt 11:30. 78. Cf. Rom 5:20. 79. Cf. Rom 7:12ff.
80. Lk 14:28ff. 81. Jas 3:2.

we are deceiving ourselves."[82] But it does not follow that we must therefore perish. Scripture consoles us saying: "If anyone sin, we have as advocate Jesus Christ the just; he himself is the atonement of our sins."[83] And the prophet too testifies to his intercession on behalf of the transgressors[84] (but note well that he speaks of transgression and not of contempt). How, I ask, can they perish for whom the Savior himself has asked forgiveness? I cannot at all see how you can attach such exaggerated weight to every disobedience and transgression of the least precept as to exclaim: "How can any sin be venial or light for a monk, when his every least action exposes him to the peril of grave disobedience?" You seem to think this is the inescapable consequence of attributing divine authority to human superiors;[85] as if even the precepts of the Gospel did not vary in weight and hence admit of degrees of merit and guilt.

The penalty is to be proportioned to the gravity of the fault

XI. 25. Furthermore, since not all commands are equally necessary, useful, or important, so the corresponding offenses vary in degree of guilt and are not to be stamped with the same stigma. An equal fault cannot be committed unless an equal obligation has been neglected; and only then is an equal punishment forthcoming. See in the Gospel how both the sin of gluttony and the vice of fornication are condemned,[86] yet who is not more repelled by the filth of fornication than by mere overeating? Has not Truth himself distinguished for us in the Gospel between grave and light disobedience by calling the one a "beam" and the other a "splinter?"[87] Has he not also demonstrated, or rather defined for us various degrees of guilt, affirming that one fault is liable to judgment, another to the council, and a third to the fire of hell?[88] Why then

82. 1 Jn 1:8.   83. 1 Jn 2:1f.   84. Cf. Is 53:12.
85. Cf. RB 5:4.   86. Cf. Lk 21:34; Mt 5:27f.; 15:19.
87. Cf. Mt 7:3ff.; Lk 6:41f.   88. Cf. Mt 5:22.

need it follow that if their spiritual masters are granted a share in divine authority, monks can therefore no longer commit light or venial sins, or that their every least act exposes them to the peril of grave disobedience? Certainly there is a class of sin to which is assigned this hell of punishment, or punishment of hell, but what of that other, which Divine Truth has let off with a mere summons to judgment? We cannot say he is not guilty after his guilt has been so proclaimed, and if he is guilty he must have sinned. Now a sin is an offense against a command of God, and therefore a species of disobedience.

26. From this you may gather that it is a sin of disobedience to be "angry with your brother,"[89] but not a grave one. Behold, here is at least one venial sin a monk can commit, and he is disobeying no mere man, but God himself! We might say the same of foolish, vain, or idle words, thoughts and actions. These things are also always infractions of a law, and that law is divine. They are sins too, and hence displeasing to God; yet they are venial, not mortal, except in cases where contempt has rendered them habitual. In this last case it is still not the matter of the sin, but rather the intention of the sinner which is gravely reprehensible. The pride of contempt and the obstinacy of impenitence here render more serious the sin which in itself would be only venial and convert the light blemish of irregularity into the serious crime of rebellion.

Serious disobedience

You may find a good definition of the mortal sin of disobedience in Samuel. He says: "It is like the sin of witchcraft to rebel; and like the crime of idolatry to refuse to obey."[90] Note the wording. He does not say, "to fail to obey," but "to refuse to obey." The guilt of idolatry is imputed not to a simple failure to carry out an order, but to the proud recalcitrance of the will. Failure to obey and refusal to obey are by no means the same thing. The one may

89. *Ibid.*   90. I Kings 15:23.

arise from ignorance, or often enough from infirmity; the other rather from hateful stubbornness or unbearable contumacy. This latter rebels against and resists the Holy Spirit[91] and if it lasts until death, it is the blasphemy which cannot be forgiven in this world or the next.[92]

You see then that not every unfulfilled command involves a mortal sin of disobedience, but only recalcitrance and refusal to obey. And very often the disobedient lack this rebellious ill will. How then can a monk be so exposed to the grave peril of disobedience, when his sin cannot be mortal unless he be also rebellious and contumacious?

27. It is futile for some people to compare, as you mention, any and every disobedience to that ancient disobedience committed in Paradise,[93] which indeed not only incriminated its perpetrators, but also vitiated our human nature. I believe that also in this first and most serious disobedience, it was principally, if not solely, the rebellion and self-justification which followed that merited such a severe sentence, rather than the act itself. When God asked the reason for the sin and thus offered them an opportunity to repent (for he wills not the death, but rather the repentance of the sinner),[94] they chose rather to turn aside in evil words, excusing their sin.[95] Herein lay a twofold malice, for Adam sinned against himself in refusing to confess and win pardon, and then against his wife in cruelly accusing her in order to falsely excuse himself.[96]

28. How could you proceed to say that "the crime of grave disobedience lies in wait for the monk in his every least action?" As if such guilt could creep up on him by surprise or accident, or be forced on him by circumstances when he finds it impossible to fulfill a given order! I say now, is a monk really threatened thus by spiritual death at every turn? No! I believe God would have granted even Adam full pardon, had he but humbled himself and confessed instead of trying to justify himself. As we have seen, simple disobedience, even when deliberate, is not so serious as self-excuse and premeditated obstinacy.

91. Cf. Acts 7:51.   92. Cf. Mt 12:31–32.   93. Cf. Gen 3:9ff.
94. Cf. Ezek 33:11.   95. Cf. Ps 140:4 (Vulgate).   96. Cf. Gen 3:10ff

XII. 29. But perhaps this distinction between grave and light disobedience which applies to divine law is not valid for our Rule as well? That would be putting what is merely human above what is divine. Can God's spokesmen have more authority than their Master? Does not St Benedict himself speak of grave and of lighter faults?[97] Are not these lighter faults so many instances of lighter disobedience?

Superiors, then, issue minor commands in accord with the Rule, and when these are transgressed, the fault is a minor one, although in disobeying one's abbot one also disobeys God. Even when it is God himself who speaks, there are greater and lesser precepts which bind proportionately. The "first and greatest commandment"[98] defined by Our Lord himself must certainly be observed with greater care than those others of which he said: "He who sets aside one of these least commandments."[99] What then? Can we still speak of equally serious guilt for the transgression of any and all commands when the Rule mentions greater and lesser faults and the Gospel greater and lesser commandments? There is no need then for me to choose between the alternatives you offer me; that is either to deny divine authority to human superiors who issue legitimate commands, or to admit that monks cannot commit a venial sin. Of course, I do admit that in disobeying those who hold God's place we disobey God, provided always that they do not command anything contrary to God; however, these commands do not all require the same care in execution, nor does their infraction always entail the same guilt. Although he who is offended is the same in all these cases, the weight of what is ordered is not, and therefore the transgressions of all commands are not to be equated. Thus our Father St Benedict said: "Let the measure of excommunication be in accord with the gravity of the fault."[100]

30. You see then that it is foolish to be disturbed or to upset others on account of the obedience which you have promised according to our holy Rule, as if you should not promise something

97. Cf. RB 24; 25.
99. Mt 5:19.

98. Mt 22:38.
100. RB 24:1.

you simply can neither perform nor leave undone without grave sin, since your superior's legitimate commands are to you as those of God. Foolish, I say, thus to exaggerate the evil of disobedience to the point of deterring yourselves from embracing the most necessary good of vowed obedience. It is true, as you say, that many difficulties lie in wait for us, or creep up on us among these many and varied obligations which obedience imposes upon us, but it is not always a mortal sin or a token of perdition not to fulfill what has been commanded. All disobedience is blameworthy and inexcusable, but it is never eternally lethal unless one refuse to apply the remedy of penance. In fact, simple disobedience is never a mortal sin, unless it is joined to proud contempt. The sons of obedience[101] then have great security; that very peace promised to men of good will,[102] for one cannot be damned unless one be impenitent (which is quite impossible for those who love God),[103] nor can one sin gravely except by pride, from which the fear of hell should suffice to restrain us.

A breach of silence can be a serious sin

Perhaps an example will make all this more clear: If a superior command me to keep silence, but I let slip a word through forgetfulness, I have indeed disobeyed, but not seriously. On the other hand, should I break silence willfully and deliberately and out of contempt for the command, my offense is mortal and if I do not repent I shall be damned.

XIII. 31. Is this perhaps still too hard for you? You also said, I believe, after considering the difficulty, or as you call it, the impossibility of monastic obedience, something like the following: "Is this that road to God which is supposed to be all the safer for being strict, and all the surer for being hard? Must a monk who is as human as anyone, and who has trouble enough avoiding what is in itself evil

101. Cf. 1 Pet 1:14.   102. Cf. Lk 2:14.   103. Cf. Lk 12:5.

and in cultivating what is in its nature good, also avoid or cultivate with a like solicitude whatever his superior sees fit to forbid or command?" And you go on to say: "Since this is believed by many, but practiced by few, and that imperfectly how is such a belief any different from that freedom which the Apostle reproves in connection with the eating of food offered to idols?"[104] It would be no different indeed, if it were as you say. In fact, one would have to be out of one's mind to dare to omit what he believes himself seriously obliged to.

You believe, then, if I may sum up your argument, that the commands of God can hardly be observed, and those of one's abbot simply cannot; for Truth himself requires that not one jot be passed over.[105] If you will pardon my saying so, it seems to me that anyone who reasons thus has yet to taste the sweetness of the Lord. He still groans beneath the yoke of the law and has yet to feel the sweetness of the yoke of Christ. He has no experience of the consolations of grace and the weakness of his nature most surely holds him down, for he lacks the help of the Spirit.

32. What is the meaning of this distinction of yours? You say the commands and prohibitions of God are difficult to observe, while those of human superiors are impossible. As if one could succeed in fulfilling the one without the other! Notice that God has commanded us to obey even evil superiors, of whom he said: "All things that they command you, observe and do."[106] You see then if we disobey them, we are not merely disobeying this or that man, but God himself.

So nobody obeys his superior perfectly. I grant it, but what do you suppose is the reason? Is it because we can't or because we won't? If we want to but cannot, we may be at peace; but if we can but will not, we are guilty of pride. I agree that the caution which you mention is necessary, but only as a means of avoiding the pride which may lead to serious disobedience.

Do you perhaps think it impossible to refrain from disdaining the commands of superiors? Know that countless men have learned

104. Cf. 1 Cor 8:7ff.   105. Cf. Mt 5:18.   106. Mt 23:3; RB 4:61.

to believe otherwise by their own experience. Or would you call difficult but not impossible the self-restraint which does not despise a superior? Though pain holds in check a proud spirit, you would yet murmur against obedience and say that it is dangerous to promise what is so difficult to accomplish. Then I can only remind you of Our Lord's words: "Let him accept it who can."[107] It is this to which I was referring a little while ago when I spoke of taking stock of one's resources before commencing to build.[108] As someone has said: "Either don't try, or carry it through."[109]

Of course no one who realizes what he is saying would promise never to transgress. This would be the same as promising impeccability. One who could promise such a thing on oath would be either a perjurer, or holier than he who said: "We all offend in many things."[110] It would be well to re-examine an argument which leads to such false conclusions, lest the law which was intended to minimize faults should not only fail to do so, but should also become an occasion for perjury. That would be the situation if one thought he were promising something by his vows which he could not perform.

The Rule is divided into precepts and remedies

33. We may divide all regular observance into two categories: precepts and remedies. Precepts set us to fight against sin, whereas remedies restore us to innocence after we have fallen. These two are both integral parts of the regular life, so that if a professed brother accept the remedy offered by the Rule when he has transgressed some regulation, he has not broken his contract, although he has violated a precept. It is only when both the precept and the remedy have been scorned that I would consider the vow to be violated, the undertaking abandoned, or the contract broken. Thus I judge him safe who although he offended against obedience, has

107. Mt 19:12.   108. Cf. Lk 14:28ff.
109. Ovid, *Ars Amatium*, 1:389.   110. Jas 3:2.

not despised the remedy of penance. The limits of the Rule, however battered, are not broken so long as the discipline of regular penance is accepted. Regular correction is part of the Rule, for this Rule is not only the norm of a good life, but also the instrument for repairing what is evil. It contains both the precepts of obedience and the remedies for disobedience, so that even in sinning we escape not its care. I freely acknowledge that it is impossible for any mortal always to avoid venial faults against obedience, but that does not make our Rule impossible to observe, for it even provides remedies for serious offenses.

You were right then in saying that nobody can always obey his superiors perfectly; but disobedience is only a light fault for which the Rule provides us a ready remedy; provided, that is, that there has been no contempt involved. If you contend that this too is unavoidable, you are surely in error. Moreover, the Rule has a remedy for this more serious ill also, and although the medicine is bitter, the contract of monastic profession remains intact so long as it is not despised.

34. Such being the case, it is senseless for us who have professed this Rule to complain of impossibility; to pretend we cannot help but sin; that the just commands of religious superiors come not from God, but only from men, and may therefore be set aside. It should be plain now that our promise contains nothing impossible, although we ought to obey these men just as we would God. What professed monk does not find it possible and even easy, by God's grace, to keep his pledge, realizing that it is not by simple disobedience that he breaks it but only by impenitence? I have already mentioned that we do not promise never to fail; hence simple obedience does not constitute in itself a breach of promise, except perhaps for him who in error supposes himself obliged to that extent. You maintain that there are quite a few such people. I can only say of these, if they indeed exist, that which you yourselves have said. Their consciences suffer by this excessive credulity, self-cruelty rather,[111] in the same way that others suffered by the

---

111. A typical play on words: *credulitas, vel potius crudelitas.*

harmful freedom of those who ate what had been offered to idols. These monks of necessity perish through their own judgment, just as the Apostle declares the weak brother perishes in the other's knowledge.[112] It is the same Apostle who teaches us that no creature of God is unclean when it may be accepted with thanksgiving[113] by those who are properly instructed. It is much the same with religious profession. It cannot in itself be the cause of damnation to anyone, except to him who erroneously supposes such to be the case, and I think I have sufficiently outlined the true perspective.

St Paul on idol offerings and on the simple and the evil eye

XIV. 35. Now I turn to the difficulty caused you by this particular doctrine of the Apostle. You want to know if these words of St Paul concerning idol offerings may be taken as a general rule: "I think that nothing is unclean in Christ; but to him who regards anything as unclean, to him it is . . . if he eat, he is condemned in his bad faith."[114] Thus if anyone does a good act in the belief that it is evil, it becomes evil for him to the extent of his conviction. If I agree to this, you want to know further why the converse is not true, so that an evil act would become good to the extent that one believed it so.

You say that it seems strange and even unfair that the human understanding should be more powerful in evil than in good. If I answer that it is natural for the "evil eye" to produce an evil effect, you will probably reply that it ought to be even more natural for the "simple eye" to produce a good effect. He who said that the whole body is cast into darkness by an evil eye, also said that a simple eye made it full of light.[115] But you should ask whether the eye which is deceived is truly simple, since he who takes evil for

---

112. Cf. 1 Cor 8:7ff. 113. Cf. 1 Tim 4:4.

114. Cf. Rom 14:14, 23; Bernard's reading differs from the Vulgate, the latter giving a somewhat different meaning: "I am confident in the Lord Jesus that nothing is of itself unclean. . . ."

115. Cf. Mt 6:22f.

good is as mistaken as he who takes good for evil. Don't you see that they both incur the Prophet's curse, "Woe to you who call good evil and evil good?"[116] Let no one then try to dodge this thrust of the Prophet by quoting the words of Truth about the simple eye which is the "light" of the whole "body" of an action. God forbid that there could be any disagreement between the Herald of Truth and Truth itself, one cursing what the other approves.

36. I believe two things are necessary for the interior eye to be truly simple; that is, charity in the intention and truth in the choice. If one loves the good but does not choose the true, he has the zeal of God, but not according to knowledge.[117] Indeed I fail to see how in the judgment of Truth true simplicity can co-exist with error.

Wishing to instruct his disciples concerning true simplicity, the Master said: "Be therefore prudent as serpents and simple as doves."[118] He puts prudence first, for without it, no one can be properly simple. How can that eye be truly simple which cannot see the truth? Or indeed how can that be called true simplicity which is ignorant of the simple truth? But it is written: "The ignorant should be ignored."[119] It is plain then that this simplicity which is praised by Our Lord presupposes these two conditions: good will and prudence. A man needs not only a warm and undeceiving heart but a keen and undeceived eye as well.

37. Just as the truly simple eye requires both love of the good and knowledge of the true, so the evil eye is the result of the two opposite qualities: blindness which prevents one from recognizing the truth, and perversity which leads one to love evil. Between this double good which is neither deceitful nor deceived and this double evil which is both perverted and perverse lie two intermediate states. One of these is good, for its inner eye retains its good zeal and is not party to the deception of which it is the ignorant victim. The other is evil for although it is not opposed to the knowledge of the true, malice makes it insensible to the love of the good.

---

116. Is 5:20.   117. Cf. Rom 10:2.   118. Mt 10:16.
119. Cf. 1 Cor 14:38 (variant reading). The Vulgate text has "if anyone ignores this, let him be ignored."

38. Since all things are best understood by making distinctions, we may discern a fourfold gradation in the eye of the heart, according to this twofold evil and that double good. On the one hand we have the good and the better, and on the other the bad and the worse. But let us take a few examples. First there is the man who loves good, but does evil unwittingly. His eye is good, since he has good will, but it is not simple, because it is blind. Then there is another who both freely does the good and prudently discerns it. He has a truly simple eye, for he lacks neither quality, having both knowledge and good zeal. It is for an eye like this that God's own eye searches when he looks out over the sons of men to see if any understand or seek him.[120]

On the other hand, there is the man who does not love good, but rather hates it in his perversity. He has knowledge still, but uses it to further his evil designs. I cannot call him ignorant or blind, but I do not call him evil either, for he still has the one good of truth; though he uses it to harm himself.

39. Lastly there is the man who may do the objective good which he hates, but only by mistake. Rightly I would say he is evil, for he lacks no evil, he is both blind and perverse. He is said to be evil or empty, because he is void of any good at all,[121] without knowledge of the true or love of the good.

Concerning our first example the Prophet says: "Ephraim is like unto an ensnared dove, which has lost heart,"[122] for though he is not deceitful, he is none the less prone to be deceived. The second is that "simple eye" mentioned by the Lord when he taught the Apostles: "Be therefore wise as serpents, and simple as doves."[123] It is neither deceitful nor easily deceived.

40. It is the Lord again who says: "The children of this world are wiser in their generation than the children of light,"[124] characteriz-

---

120. Cf. Ps 14:2.

121. Bernard has here an untranslated play on words: *Dicitur siquidem nequam, quasi nequaquam, ut is solummodo nequam appelletur, qui nequaquam, hoc est, in nullo penitus, appareat bonus. . . .*

122. Hos 7:11.　　　123. Mt 10:16.　　　124. Lk 16:8.

ing thus the malice of those who deceive, but who are not themselves readily deceived. Such an eye is singly evil.

As for him whom we have called evil or empty, he is doubly evil. His malice gives birth to ignorance which in turn confounds the malice producing it. He often fails in his evil purpose and unwittingly does the good instead. "Their foolish hearts are darkened,"[125] and they are, as it were, already "delivered up to a reprobate sense,"[126] so that they cannot love or discern the good. Of these it is written, "The wicked, having plumbed the depths of sin, reach contempt,"[127] for a man like this does not wish to avoid evil if he could. Nor does he know how to avoid it, should he try. I have put him last on the list, not because his malice is greater than that of him who sins with open eyes, but because it is more dangerous. He feels secure in his ignorance, and this false security fosters torpor rather than malice. The other has but the single evil of a bad intention; this man has also a false perspective, and is certainly in a worse state. He also lacks true judgment while the other lacks only the quality of good zeal. I believe it was to him and to his opposite who possesses these two qualities which he lacks, that Truth was referring when he spoke of the simple and the evil eye which render the whole body either radiant or wrapped in darkness.[128] The other two we have mentioned have something of darkness and something of light, and hence cannot be classified as totally pervaded by either.

41. But to get back to your difficulty; if such a one is completely evil, though he does good maliciously and blindly, thinking it to be evil, this good act of his becomes actually evil for him to the extent of his mistaken belief. That is what Our Lord meant by saying that his whole body is dark.[129] What light can remain where both good intention and true judgment are lacking? But it does not follow from this that he who does evil, thinking it to be good, is therefore credited with a good act. How so? It is because his eye is not simple as required by the word of Truth, in order for the whole body of his

125. Rom 1:21. 126. Rom 1:28. 127. Prov 18:3.
128. Cf. Mt 6:22f. 129. *Ibid.*

K

act to be clothed with the light of goodness,[130] as we have already outlined. In fact, it has an element of darkness, for ignorance clouds over the light of its good will. Since the other has both kinds of evil, but this one only one kind of good, it follows that the former is more powerful in evil than the latter in doing good. One good quality cannot counterbalance two evil qualities.

I admit, of course, that the good intention is praiseworthy and that the good will does not lose its due reward in spite of the evil it has done; yet the simplicity which can be so deceived is certainly tinged with evil. "But," you may protest, "was it not done in good faith?" In faith indeed, but in false faith; or rather in no faith, for false faith is really not faith at all. In fact, I believe the Apostle was referring to true faith only and not to false faith when he said, "All that is not of faith is sin."[131] True faith can never take evil for good, for that would be falsehood and hence a species of sin. This text, "All that is not of faith is sin," may be applied to both blind malice and erring innocence, because on the one hand anything done in ignorance, even if it might be good in itself, is totally vitiated by an evil intention. On the other hand a good intention does not suffice to completely excuse an act which is evil.

Therefore, if you perform an evil act in the belief that it is good or a good act in the belief that it is evil, you have sinned in either case, since you have not acted in faith. However, the sin would certainly be lighter in the case of an outwardly evil act done with an upright intention than when an apparently good act is done with an evil intention. Still any act which has the least taint of evil is not fully good. How then can such a defective good have an efficacy comparable to that of pure evil, so that the one should counterbalance the other?

Enough now on this matter. As to those questions you may think I am ignoring, I believe I have already sufficiently answered them. You often twist the same question about and repeat it with but slight variations, and I see no need of going into all that. Even when a question has been repeated over and over, a single answer is all that is required.

130. Cf. Mt 6:22.   131. Rom 14:23.

The proportionate merit and gravity of obedience and disobedience

XV. 42. However, since your main question was about the obligations of obedience and the various sorts of disobedience, we may go into the side question you raised concerning the merit of these; that is, whether the evil of disobeying a given precept be proportionate to the good of fulfilling it. For example, Abraham's sacrifice of his son,[132] or that nameless father who is said to have risked his son's life in a fiery furnace;[133] would these holy men have merited a measure of divine wrath and chastisement proportionate to the praise and the favor they actually gained, had they failed to obey? You are of the opinion that such is the case though you consider it severe, but you are wrong.

There are certain acts which merit glory when performed, but which can be omitted without fault. Consequently, if they are done they are fittingly rewarded, but if they are not done, there is no punishment. For instance, it is no little virtue not to touch a woman,[134] but if a man embrace his own wife there is surely no fault in it. Under this heading fall all those evangelical counsels to which are aptly applied the words: "Let him accept it who can."[135]

43. On the other hand there are acts which cannot be omitted without sin, but which are no particular credit to their authors. Those who scorn them will perish, but those who perform them get no glory. Such are the precepts of the natural law, binding on all men, and without which no one can be saved. Even the gentiles had a saying about it: " 'I am no robber,' he said; and I answered, 'Then you need not feed the crows from the cross.' "[136] So too the Gospel: "If you love those who love you, what reward shall you have? And if you salute your brethren only, what are you doing more than others?"[137] And again in more general terms, "When

---

132. Cf. Gen 22.   133. Cf. *Vitae Patrum*, 5:14:18 (PL 73:952).
134. Cf. 1 Cor 7:1.   135. Mt 19:12.
136. Horace, *Epistolae*, 1:16:46ff., trans. E. Wickham, *Horace for English Readers* (London: Oxford University Press, 1930), p. 300.
137. Mt 5:46f.

you have done everything that was commanded you, say, 'We are unprofitable servants who have only done our duty.' "[138] It is as if he had said: "If you are content with the precepts and customs imposed upon you by law without freely embracing my counsels and recommendations for perfection, you have done your duty, but you are hardly heroes; you have escaped punishment, but won no crown."

How then need we feel compelled to fear a chastisement for our every disobedience proportionate to the reward we may hope to win by obedience? On the contrary, we may take it as a general rule in these matters, that if the thing commanded is difficult, the merit of obedience exceeds the guilt of refusal, but that if the matter is easy the guilt of disobedience outweighs the merit of compliance.

The promise of local Stability

WVI. 44. Now if we may take that as settled, we can proceed to examine that local stability to which we commit ourselves at profession and to determine what, if any, circumstances would postulate or justify our changing it. It seems you also have some difficulty on this point.

I may now confidently reply that one is never justified in defaulting when he has promised by vow to do a good act. Hence, I would never advise anyone to abandon the place which he has freely chosen and where he has promised with his own lips to remain; nor would St Gregory, for he says: "Even a perfect man will watch himself very carefully, lest he lapse into some less perfect thought or deed."[139]

What this apostolic man felt, that the Apostle was proud to see fulfilled in himself, as he said: "Forgetting what is behind, I strain forward to what is ahead."[140] Does not the Prophet Ezekiel express the same idea in his description of the living creatures: "They never went backward when they moved, but each marched straight

138. Lk 17:10.
139. St Gregory, *On Ezekiel*, 1:9 (PL 76:814b).   140. Phil 3:13.

ahead."[141] All these are of like mind, for they are the servants of him who said: "No man having put his hand to the plow and looking back, is fit for the kingdom of God."[142]

The contract of stability then, rules out henceforth any feeble relapse, angry departure, aimless or curious wandering, and every vagary of fickleness; but it does not rule out what the monk promises with his next breath in the formula of profession. I mean conversion of manners and obedience according to the Rule. If he is impeded in observing these by the irreligious and vicious habits of his brethren, I would counsel him to remove to some other place under the guidance of the Spirit of liberty, where he may be more free to live as he has engaged himself by vow to do. Indeed, with the holy, one may become holy, but with the perverse, perverted.[143]

45. For all that, I would never advise any member of a proper and well regulated monastery, even out of a desire for a stricter observance, to change his residence without permission from his superiors. Should one have already done this, however, and settled himself in a more perfect life, I would then counsel him to remain and not return to the less perfect life he has relinquished for something better; the more so if he is better able to fulfill his original vows in the second monastery than in the first. Let him remind himself of his motive and purpose in undertaking this stricter or more perfect life. I could never counsel him to return to the less perfect, for that would be a species of apostasy — that is unless he has not gone far, for in that case the Rule is clear: a monk from a known monastery cannot be kept or even received without the consent of his abbot.[144] But let me illustrate these things by giving a concrete example.

46. Suppose a monk of the Cluniac observance wishes to embrace the more austere poverty of the Cistercians, considering that there he may find a purer observance of the Rule without the accretions of so many customs. Should he ask my opinion I would discourage him, at least if he did not have the consent of his abbot in this design of his.

---

141. Ezek 1:9 (cf. n. 139).   142. Lk 9:62.
143. Ps 18:26.   144. RB 61:13.

Why? Well, first of all, to prevent any scandal to those whom he would be leaving. Secondly, because it is hardly safe to leave a certain good for an uncertain hope. Perhaps he will not be able to measure up to the higher standard, whereas he is now within his capacity. Thirdly, I should be on my guard against instability of character in such a one, for that which one lightly desires when he does not have it may well become insupportable once experienced. This sort of foolish levity is only too common, for people unreasonably want a thing one moment and reject it the next. How many do we not see who can scarcely abide in one mind a single hour? Propelled by the winds of their fancy, they flit here and there as if intoxicated, changing their minds at every turn, or rather floating about without any mind at all. Every place they go, they come up with new plans and projects, always desiring what they have not, and sick of what is now in their grasp.

47. Someone perhaps will inquire, "But how can I with a good conscience live a life which is not in full accord with the Rule I have professed? If I do not keep my vow, am I not a perjurer?" As if there would not be even more grounds for complaint elsewhere once you had begun to live completely according to the Rule. Yes, even then you would be asking, "How can I bear to live outside of my original monastery with a quiet conscience—that harbor which sheltered me when I first fled from the world, which instructed me in the paths of virtue and set me on the road to salvation! How can I thus offend my brethren, disobey my father, and to crown all, break my promise of stability, playing false to my first loyalty?"

But truly, I say, neither of these complaints is just. He who thinks it perjury not to observe the Rule in its purity, has I think, paid scant attention to what he actually promised. No one at profession really promises "the Rule," but specifically, that he will act "according to the Rule" in the inception and pursuit of his holy undertaking. This sort of profession formula has, in our day, been adopted by almost all monks. However, God is served in many diverse ways in the various monasteries. So long as one carefully observes the good customs of his house he is beyond any doubt living according to the Rule, for the Rule admits of variations in local customs.

Whoever then holds fast to the good which he finds ready at hand in the place where he has made profession is certainly living as he had promised, for this was doubtless his intention when he pronounced his vows: to imitate and share in the virtuous life of the brethren of that monastery.

48. What then? Must the monks of Tours[145] adopt the customs of Cluny, or should Cluny give place to Tours? Would you perhaps have both adopt the strict literal interpretation of Cîteaux? We have indeed all professed the same Rule, and even in the very same words, but since the implicit intention is different in each case, different observances can undoubtedly be followed in different places without fear of perjury or perdition. Even among good Christians, everybody does not keep everything in the Gospel, although they all live according to the Gospel. Thus those who are content to contract a legitimate marriage do not feel that they have abandoned the Gospel in not choosing to follow the sublime counsel of celibacy, that is, as long as they faithfully fulfill the duties of their own state. It is so too with those who undertake to live according to the Rule. Even if they do not keep it all "to a hair" (as the saying goes), and even if they change or omit certain details according to the customs of their house, as long as they are faithful to what is locally accepted as a "sober, just and pious life,"[146] they are truly living the Rule. Such conduct is, in fact, recommended by the Rule itself in the eighth degree of humility: "That a monk do nothing that is not sanctioned by the customs of the house, or the example of the seniors."[147]

49. Of course, it is a different matter for the Cistercians and for those who, like them, have promised an integral literal observance of the Rule rather than life according to the Rule, since such is their interpretation of monastic profession.

---

145. Lit. "in the Great Monastery," *in Maiore Monasteria*. The reference is to the proto-monastery near Tours which looks back to St Martin as its founder.

146. Tit 2:12.   147. RB 7:55.

For the rest, let no one be disturbed by his solemn profession according to the Rule so long as he is faithful to obedience, for he has not promised to observe the Rule in its entirety. This is valid at least for those monasteries where the local customs are based on good order and discipline. Let the proper interpretation of profession be maintained in each monastery, safeguarding what is proper to each and provided that an upright intention be also maintained.

If anyone, still unquiet and dissatisfied with this reasoning, would give way to the prompting of conscience and leave his monastery in search of some better means of accomplishing what he considers himself to have promised and thus far defaulted in, I could not approve his departure, but neither would I urge his return, so long as he has withdrawn to a distant and unknown house.

Why so? Both because of the Pauline pronouncement regarding the blessedness of him "who does not condemn himself by what he approves,"[148] and because of the authority of our Legislator who orders such a one to be received and kept. In fact, if he be found good and helpful, it is recommended that he be kept for good: "Let him be then persuaded to stay on."[149]

Lest such a one be disturbed later by the usual scruples concerning his former house and his broken promise, our Father goes on to console him with these wise words: "For we everywhere serve the one God and fight for the one King."[150] However, what is recommended in the case of a pilgrim monk is forbidden in the case of a neighbor; lest there be matter for scandal and friction between neighboring monasteries if they receive each other's monks without mutual consent. Our own experience has repeatedly proven the folly of presuming to set aside this provision of the Rule.

50. If then, a brother has been thus regularly incorporated into another monastery and is nonetheless disquieted by the remembrance of the scandal he may have caused to his former brethren, proposing to repair the fault by returning, let him reflect that it is of no profit to substitute one scandal for another. What sort of a remedy is it to repair one scandal by creating another? Indeed the

148. Rom 14:22   149. RB 61:9.   150. RB 61:10.

first scandal is more bearable than the projected apostasy and more easily forgiven, since it was occasioned by praiseworthy intentions. Certainly it was safer to follow your conscience, in spite of the scandal, in what you considered to be better, than to stay in your first place and profession against your conscience; although you could do that too if you could convince your conscience.

51. I can think of no better conclusion to this little discussion than to refer you again to the judgment of the Apostle concerning scandals in eating. If one brother is impelled by conscience to change his house in order (as he sees it) not to break his vows, let him not therefore despise those who remain behind; if another stands fast in good faith and fraternal unity and avoids scandalizing his brethren, let him not judge the former.[151] Here you have the best solution which I can offer to this question, although perhaps someone else may be able to offer you a better one.

XVII. 52. You would have me explain why St Gregory permitted a certain brother Venard to return to the sacraments as a secular after having spurned the monastic habit which he had formerly worn with piety.[152] Also you want to know how St Augustine could put the law of matrimony before the vow of chastity, since he seems to hold in his book on virginity[153] that the matrimonial contract is to be considered as indissolubly binding even for those who have bound themselves by vow to a life of evangelical chastity and subsequently, deceived by the devil, have broken their vows and married.

For the present I see no clearer or briefer answer to these questions than to say that this is what these holy Bishops maintain. Let

---

151. Cf. Rom 14:3.

152. Cf. St Gregory, *Letter* 43, bk. 6 (PL 77:830); trans. J. Barmby, *Selected Epistles of St Gregory the Great* (*Nicene and Post-Nicene Fathers,* second series, New York: Christian Literature, 1895), vol. 12, p. 201. There are eight other letters dealing with this Venard or Venantius, his wife and daughters (cf. *op. cit.,* p. 84).

153. Cf. St Augustine, "On the Good of Widowhood," 13f. (PL 40:438 seq.); trans. C. Cornish, *The Works of St Augustine* (*Nicene and Post-Nicene Fathers,* first series New York: Charles Scribner's Sons, 1905), vol. 3, p. 446.

them answer for themselves whether they are right. When there is any question concerning the opinions or deeds of the Fathers, I hold fast to that saying of the Apostle: that among dispensers we should seek a man who is trustworthy.[154] I am quite sure that whether they spoke under divine inspiration or on their own authority, they are as trustworthy in this instance as in any other; the one in disposing the matter before him, the other in writing what he thought.

53. Then you asked about those bishops whom the same Pope Gregory commanded to live for a time in a monastery because of their excesses.[155] Did they wear the holy habit, or their ordinary clothes? I simply do not know, but it seems credible that the habit would not have been given to transients who sought only quiet in the seclusion of the monastery and an opportunity for penance.

Monastic life: a second baptism

54. You have also asked my opinion on monastic profession considered as a second baptism. Why has our way of life rather than other penitential callings merited the prerogative of this appellation? I think it is because of the more perfect renouncement of the world and the singular excellence of such a spiritual way of life. It makes those who live it and love it stand out from other men as rivals of the angels and as hardly men at all; for it restores the divine image in the human soul and makes us Christlike, much as baptism does. It is also like another baptism in that we mortify the earthly side of our nature,[156] so that we may be more and more clothed with Christ,[157] being thus again "buried in the likeness of his death."[158] Just as in baptism we are delivered from the power of darkness and carried over into the kingdom of light,[159] so likewise in the second regeneration of this holy profession we are refashioned in the light of virtue, being delivered, not now from

154. 1 Cor 4:2. 155. St Gregory, *Letter* 45, bk. 13 (PL 77:1294c).
156. Cf. Col 3:5. 157. Cf. Gal 3:27. 158. Rom 6:5.
159. Cf. Col 1:13.

the unique darkness of original sin, but from many actual sins, according to that cry of the Apostle: "The night is far advanced, and the day is at hand."[160]

Whether a change of abbot favors a change of monastery

XVIII. 55. You have also asked to be enlightened as to whether a change of abbot might favor the design of a monk who wishes to change his monastery; that is, whether the death or resignation of a superior in any way affects the freedom of his subjects, so that during the interval before a successor is named they might go where they please. To this I reply: by no means! After all, the promise of profession when made according to custom in the oratory takes the abbot's presence as its witness, not his life as its term. Let the term of the contract be the monk's own life, not someone else's.

Listen now to what our Legislator has both thought and written: "If he ever do otherwise," that is other than he has promised, "let him know that he will be condemned by God, whom he mocks."[161] Again he says that the monk "is not to have even his own body henceforth at his free disposal,"[162] and in another place he speaks of "persevering in the monastery until death."[163]

Except then for the special cases which have been outlined above, let no monk ever forsake the house of his profession during his life-time, at least not by his own choice. Otherwise he stands self-condemned, having broken his solemn word.

Which is safer for a monk: to remain in bitterness or to seek peace elsewhere?

56. But you go on to plead consideration for special difficulties: "What if one be unable to remain without constant rancor in his heart, due to an unhappy or irregular election of the new abbot?"

160. Rom 13:12.   161. RB 63:18.   162. RB 33:4; 58:25.
163. RB, Prol. 50.

I am reminded now of the Gospel scene where Our Lord instructs the Apostles concerning the obligations of matrimony, whereupon they exclaim, "If such be the case, it is not expedient to marry!"[164] Indeed, it is a difficult matter: nothing could be more burdensome than to live with a hateful woman, but it would be most unchristian to break up the marriage.

It is much the same with a monk who cannot abide in his monastery lest he die of mental strain induced by rancor, and cannot depart either, lest he break his vow. What counsel can I give to such a person? That he leave? But that would be unlawful because of his profession. That he stay? That would not do, because of his rancor. You offer me two things equally dangerous and unhappy, so that whatever I reply, it will not be to your profit. You ask which is safer for a monk, to remain with rancor in his own monastery under an illegitimate superior or to seek peace elsewhere. It is rather as if one who had determined on suicide were to ask me if he should throw himself into the fire or over the precipice. He burns indeed who lives in hate, and he falls fatally who breaks his vow.

Perhaps my best exit from this dilemma is to follow the lead of your subsequent remarks. You say that by "irregular election" you mean one which is so tangled and involved that, although it is doubtless invalid in God's eyes, its invalidity is difficult if not impossible to prove to the satisfaction of men. I am reminded now of that saying in Proverbs: "He who would abandon a friend seeks a pretext."[165] How can you call an election irregular if you cannot prove it? Have you never heard the saying: "If it can't be proven, it is nothing to me?"

"But," you will plead, "how can I obey one whom I know to be unworthy, even though the facts are not public?" My brethren, have you never read in your Rule that Rule of Truth which says: "The scribes and pharisees have sat on the chair of Moses; . . . do what they tell you, but do not act according to their example?"[166]

---

164. Mt 19:10.   165. Prov 18:1.   **166.** Mt 23:3; RB 4:61.

XIX. 57. As to changing your clothes or washing them when they have been defiled during the night, I will be brief in my reply. I would advise each one to follow the practice of his own house in these matters, for such customs vary considerably. Concerning these customs which are observed in most monasteries and which I had almost forgotten about, I think what I have said above on diverse customs in relation to stability can be applied here as well; so there is no need to repeat.

I will pass over several of your legal questions, for such things do not pertain to monks, and you can easily look them up yourselves if you care to take the trouble.

Should an angry person approach the altar?

58. I come now to those three questions contained in your other letter, the first of which amounts to this: How would you advise a person who is angry with another, not to the extent of wishing to harm him, but yet enough so that he would be glad to see harm befall this person? May one approach the altar in these dispositions, or should one rather stay away until the disturbance has passed?

I can only say that I hope I will never find myself going to the altar of peace in such a state, or partaking with wrath and quarrelsomeness of the sacrament in which God is unquestionably present, "reconciling the world to himself."[167] If God will not receive my gift until I have restored peace to any brother whom I may remember having offended,[168] how much less will he do so if I haven't even restored peace within myself.

Saint Paul: "Our conversation is in heaven. . . ."

XX. 59. Your next question is on the apparent disparity between the two Pauline texts: "Our conversation is in heaven,"[169] and, "So

167. 2 Cor 5:19.   168. Cf. Mt 5:24.   169. Phil 3:20.

long as we remain in the body, we are exiled from the Lord."[170] How can the soul be exiled from the Lord in the body, and at the same time be in heaven with the Lord? The Apostle himself gives the answer elsewhere, saying: "For we know in part and we prophesy in part."[171] In so far as we have this knowledge, contemplating these things as present, we are already with the Lord, but to the extent that we prophesy of what is yet beyond, abiding in faith and hope, rather than in understanding and vision, we know bodily exile.

"But when that which is perfect has come," that is, the light of glory which shall be ours in the resurrection, "then that which is only partial shall be done away with,"[172] that is, all the bodily infirmities which accompany our present prolonged exile in the body. It was these last he was bemoaning when he lamented: "Unhappy man that I am, who will deliver me from the body of this death?"[173] Notice that he does not complain of the body as such, but of the body "of this death," that is in its present state of corruption, showing that the body itself is not the cause of its exile, but rather its infirmities.

Again we read that, "The corruptible body weighs down the soul."[174] Note well that this is said of the "corruptible" body rather than simply of the body, since it is the corruption which constitutes the burden. Consequently, those who groan within themselves, await not the loss, but the liberation of their bodies.[175] Weighed down then, not with the companionship, but rather with the infirmities of this body, we wish to be dissolved and to be with Christ,[176] so that our partial exile may be terminated and that the partial beatitude which we have commenced to enjoy may become perfect.

60. One may also connect the words, "Our conversation is in heaven,"[177] with that other saying of the Apostle, "We are saved by hope."[178] Therefore it is hope which allows us to dwell already in heaven, while our bodies are yet in exile.

170. 2 Cor 5:6.   171. 1 Cor 13:9.   172. 1 Cor 13:10.
173. Rom 7:24.   174. Wis 9:15.   175. Cf. Rom 8:23.
176. Cf. Phil 1:23. 177. Phil. 3:20.   178. Rom 8:24.

Again one might say that we are partly bound to our bodies and partly to the Lord: bound to our bodies by bonds of life and feeling, and bound to the Lord by faith and love. Yes, love, for the soul abides no less in what it loves than in what it animates; unless perhaps unwilling necessity is considered to be a stronger bond than free and ardent choice. Indeed, "Where your treasure is, there also is your heart."[179] Again, if the soul lives by the love of God just as the body lives by the soul, how I ask can one contend that it is more present where it gives life than where it receives it? Love is the fountain of life, and the soul which does not drink from it cannot be said to live. But how could it drink if it were far from this fountain, this love, which is its God?[180]

It follows then that he who loves God is with God according to the measure of his love.[181] Insofar as he fails to love, to that extent he is yet in exile. He shows less love of God when he is occupied with bodily necessities. Indeed what is this occupation with the things of the body, but a certain absence from the Lord? If we are absent, are we not in exile? Precisely, in bodily exile from the Lord. Our intention is encumbered by the needs of the body and our love is wearied by its care.

The Gospel saying: "Your reward is great in heaven."

61. Towards the end of your second letter you ask what I think is meant by that Gospel promise, "Behold, your reward is great in heaven."[182] It seems your curiosity has been aroused by St Augustine's comment[183] that this does not refer to any visible or material heaven, nor is our reward to be found in any passing or

---

179. Mt 6:21.   180. Cf. 1 Jn 4:8, 16.

181. We have here one of St Bernard's more beautiful epigrams: *Praesens igitur Deo est qui Deum amat in quantum amat.*

182. Lk 6:23.

183. Cf. St Augustine, "Our Lord's Sermon on the Mount," 1:15 (PL 34:1236 seq.); trans. W. Findlay, *The Works of St Augustine* (Nicene and Post-Nicene Fathers, first series, New York: Charles Scribner's Sons, 1905), vol. 6, p. 8.

changeable thing, but that the reference is to some spiritual heaven for which, you say, you don't even know where to look.

But note well these words: "The Kingdom of God is within you,"[184] and "Christ dwells by faith in your hearts,"[185] that is, as a king in his own realm. Again, "The sufferings of this time are unworthy to be compared to the glory that shall be revealed in us."[186] He does not say that it will be shown to us, as if it were something outside of us, but he says "in us," hinting thus that it is already there, but as yet invisible. And again, "All the beauty of the King's daughter is within,"[187] or yet again, "Man shall come to a deep heart,"[188] for he "has arranged steps in this heart."[189] Finally, "The just soul is the seat of Wisdom"[190] for that is doubtless the meaning of the text, "Heaven is my throne."[191]

So now if you will ponder these and many other similar passages in Scripture, you will learn that the kingdom of God and his justice are to be sought within your own souls rather than outside of or above them. I am here using the terms "outside" and "above" in their literal sense; as for instance heaven is outside the earth, and the sun, the moon, and the stars are above it. For the realities which are within us in virtue of the subtlety of their invisible nature are also above us in the sublime dignity of their excellence and outside of us in the immensity of their majesty. But these are deep matters and would require more careful study, not to mention a more studious writer and a longer work.

I had hoped to confine myself to the limits of a letter in discussing these matters, but I now perceive that I have already exceeded that measure. You may consequently call this a book rather than a letter if it so pleases you. Long or short, I felt obliged to give you some reply, and I have done my best.

---

184. Lk 17:21.   185. Eph 3:17.   186. Rom 8:18.
187. Ps 44:14 (Vulgate).   188. Ps 63:7 (Vulgate).   189. Ps 83:6 (Vulgate).
190. A variant reading of Prov 12:23: "The clever man hides wisdom," which St Gregory cites as: "The just soul is the seat of Wisdom," in his Thirty-eighth Gospel Homily (PL 76:1282).
191. Is 66:1.

MONASTIC LITURGY

PROLOGUE TO THE CISTERCIAN
ANTIPHONARY

INTRODUCTION

O F THE SEVERAL DOCUMENTS connected with the Cistercian chant reform conducted under St Bernard's aegis sometime not long before 1147, only one authentic document bears his name, i.e., the *Prologus in Antiphonarium quod Cistercienses canunt ecclesiae*. The title *Prologus* is well attested by the earliest and best manuscripts; but it falls short of an adequate description of this document written by Bernard as an introduction to the reformed Cistercian Antiphonary of ca. 1147. Redacted according to the norms of twelfth-century curial documents, our *Prologus* is actually nothing less than the official act of promulgation of the reformed Antiphonary.

Every such official act required in the body of the text a summary historical account providing the pertinent background for an understanding of the object of the act, which was expressed in the *dispositio*, or concluding section of the document. Thus, Bernard's *Prologus* can be expected to provide us with at least a few details useful for our understanding of the liturgical reform in which he figured.

Date

No date of promulgation is specified in our document, and General Chapter records are too lacunose to be of help in providing a precise year. Thanks to the twelfth-century *Life* of St Stephen of

Obazine, written by a disciple of the hero, we may settle on a
year in the vicinity of 1147. According to the author, Stephen
and his colony of erstwhile hermits organized their community
life along the lines of the flourishing Cistercian Order, while
remaining quite independent of it juridically. As early as 1142, they
had received a set of Cistercian liturgical books. Only a half-decade
later, in 1147, Stephen's community was officially received into the
Order. But the Cistercian books of Obazine now had to be revised,
since they no longer conformed with the Order's recently reformed
liturgy. Thus, the Bernardine reform must have been effected
sometime between 1142 and 1147.[1]

Manuscripts and editions

The relative rarity of manuscripts is easily explained. Though the
body of chant books often remained relatively unchanged for
centuries, calendars making up the first folios underwent a continual evolution, calling at times for replacement with new folios.
Thus, many liturgical books are often found to lack the initial
folios of the original manuscript. Since our *Prologus* was meant to
appear on the very first folio, its disappearance from many antiphonary manuscripts was all but inevitable. Still, a sufficient number
of manuscripts from the twelfth and later centuries have survived
to allow for the establishment of a critical text by Dom Jean Leclercq
and Dom H. M. Rochais, *S. Bernardi Opera*, III (Rome, 1963),
pp. 515–516 (with introductory notes, pp. 511–513). Though the
text contains more than one difficult phrase, variants are few and
insignificant.

Of the eight manuscripts listed in the elenchus of manuscripts,
op. cit., pp. 512–513, only four are from the twelfth and
thirteenth centuries:

---

1. Cf. *Vita beati Stephani abbatis monasterii Obazinensis*, the twelfth-century
Life referred to above, but first edited only in 1683, by Etienne Baluze. In the
same editor's later edition, the pertinent passage from ch. 13 of bk. II may be
read in his *Miscellanea*, I, (Lucca, 1761), p. 161.

Mount Melleray, 12th c. Antiphonary from Hauterive
(Switzerland), f.1. The text has been edited by H. Séjalon,
Nomasticon Cisterciense, Solesmes, 1892, p. 244.

Cambridge, Jesus College, Ms. 34, f.109. A 12th c. collection
of "varia" from the library of Rievaulx.

Heiligenkreuz, Ms. 20, f.1. 12th/13th c. Antiphonary.

Paris, Bibliothèque Nationale, Ms. lat. 16662, f.70^v. 13th c.
collection of musical treatises, once in the possession of the
Sorbonne. The text was used by J. Hommey, in his *Supplementum Patrum*, Paris, 1684, pp. 5–6.

The version in PL 182: 1121–1122, is the non-critical (but good)
edition prepared by Dom Mabillon with the help of a transcript
sent by Cardinal Bona.

The present translation is based, of course, on the excellent text
established by Dom Leclercq and Dom Rochais, which renders
obsolete the other above-mentioned editions (as well as the poorer
editions left unmentioned).

The place of the Prologus

The manuscripts link the *Prologus* intimately with the *Praefatio*
immediately following in all manuscripts, and mentioned specifically in the final paragraph of the *Prologus*. This *Praefatio* is something
of a treatise on Cistercian chant theory, and explains in a fair amount
of detail the musical principles operative in the reform of the
primitive chant books of the Order. Similar in spirit, though more
utilitarian in purpose, is the *Tonale*, often juxtaposed with the
preceding two opuscula, and serving as a practical catechism of the
Cistercian psalm-tones and other similar formulae.[2] Since antiphonaries of the period preceding the Bernardine reform have not

---

2. The most accessible edition of the *Praefatio* is found in PL 182:1121–1132.
Typographical errors further confuse the poor edition. The *Tonale* is likewise
found in the same volume, col. 1153–1166, no less badly edited. The manuscripts present two recensions of the *Tonale*, one considerably longer than the
other. These treatises deserve better editions.

been known to be extant, the *Prologus* together with the *Praefatio* and the *Tonale* have been the chief sources drawn upon for a knowledge of the Order's chant prior to the reform.

The Prologus *description of the Cistercian reform*

Though almost every phrase invites attention, only a few specific points may be mentioned within the limits of this introduction to the text. For a more ample treatment of the material under discussion, together with select bibliographical references, see the paper by the author of this introduction, "The Origin and Early Evolution of the Cistercian Antiphonary: Reflections of Two Cistercian Chant Reforms," in *The Cistercian Spirit: A Symposium* (Cistercian Studies Series, 3).

Bernard begins by speaking of an *initial* antiphonary reform inaugurated at an early but unspecified date by the "Fathers, that is to say, those who began (*inchoatores*) the Cistercian Order." In Archbishop Hugh of Lyon's official Act regulating the details of Robert's return to Molesme, special mention is made of the liturgical books brought from Molesme to New Monastery. These books are to be kept by the pioneer monks, with the exception of a certain breviary which may be retained for purposes of transcription only until the Feast of St John the Baptist.[3] Evidently there was a certain continuity, then, in the Molesme and primitive New Monastery liturgical repertory (however much the style of celebration may have differed). How long did this continuity perdure? Impossible to say. The first-generation monks, in keeping with their thirst for the most "authentic," abandoned the Molesme books for the tradition embodied in the Metz Antiphonary. "Authentic" is here a key word of central importance. While

3. The text of Hugh's letter, embodying the decisions taken at the Colloquy of Pont-d'Anselle in 1099, forms ch. 7 of the *Exordium Parvum*, which has been frequently edited. An English translation can be found in L. Lekai, *The White Monks* (Okauchee, Wis., 1953), pp. 255ff.

certainly including present day connotations of "genuine" and "meaningful," emphasis lay rather, in the twelfth and thirteenth centuries, on "authentic" as "authoritative, because of conformity with the original."[4]

For the early Cistercians as for their coevals, "authentic antiphonary" and "Gregorian antiphonary" were convertible terms. Indeed, it is only in relatively recent times that Pope St Gregory's role in the codification of the chant we style "Gregorian" has come in for reappraisal. In the twelfth century, John the Deacon's ninth-century account of Gregory transcribing the chant melodies under direct inspiration of the Holy Spirit (in the form of a dove) was accepted as standard doctrine.

Where were "authentic" antiphonaries to be found? Bernard tells us that the Cistercian Fathers went to Metz. It was, indeed, Metz which, in the eighth century and later, had been the center of diffusion for the Roman liturgy imported by Pippin, Charlemagne, and their successors. It was held that the early tradition linked with Gregory's name was still alive and flourishing in Metz.

Yet the early Cistercians, Bernard tells us, were sadly disillusioned. The *Prologus* describes the Metz texts and melodies as "corrupt (*vitiosum*), quite badly structured (*incompositum nimis*), and deserving of contempt in almost every respect (*ac paene per omnia contemptibile*)." Harsh words. Some scholars have thought that the negative judgment simply reflects a lack of knowledge about the *real* chant. The Cistercian critics, malformed in their attitude towards chant by the bizarre musical theory of the twelfth century, simply did not recognize as authentic what was, in actual fact, a pure expression of the very best tradition. This opinion, unfortunately, is based on mere conjecture; and a serious study of the twelfth–thirteenth century chant of Metz reveals that, while there was a very homo-

---

4. For an extensive treatment of *authenticum* and correlative terms, see M. D. Chenu OP, *Introduction à S.-Thomas* (Montréal-Paris, 1950), pp. 110ff. This treatment of the word in the thirteenth-century context differs in little from the same author's discussion of twelfth-century usage, in *La théologie au douzieme siècle, Etudes de Philosophie Médiévale* 45 (Paris, 1957), pp. 351–365, where the period studied is precisely the one under scrutiny.

genous tradition at Metz, with many indications of archaic elements, the chant had nevertheless evolved along the lines of a chant "dialect." It differed considerably from what passed as "standard" in most of France and Northern Italy, and—though most of our documentation is from the thirteenth century—must have already reached a rather bad state by the twelfth century.

In spite of the negative reaction, the Metz chants were adopted (because of their "authority"?). At last the suffering became too acute, and the Abbots of the General Chapter, Bernard writes, entrusted him with the revision of the Order's Antiphonary.

Bernard mentions no one by name, but he *does* specify that he invoked the help of those of the brethren (the antecedent is "Abbots of the Chapter") with a competence in the theory and practice of the chant. He notes, too, that the reformed Antiphonary derives from many different sources (*de multis et diversis*).

After the legal clause of promulgation, there follows the directive to the effect that the interested reader should study the following Preface for further information about the reformed Antiphonary. Not surprisingly, until recently, it has been taken for granted that the principles discussed in the Preface adequately cover the program of revision. Scholars commenting on the Cistercian musical reform inevitably study only those instances evidently involving the application of the chant principles exposed in this interesting presentation of medieval chant theory. Since these principles are now recognized as artificial and incompatible with the true nature of the traditional repertory, it follows that Bernard and his fellow-editors are seen as perpetrators of a systematic mutilation of the authentic Mass and Office chants.

It is now possible, however, to get a clearer picture of the reform. With the help of several Metz manuscripts, together with an almost complete composite twelfth-century Cistercian antiphonary predating the Bernardine reform, but corrected according to the later reformed chant version, the earlier Cistercian Office chants can be reconstructed with a high degree of scientific accuracy in most instances. A collation of the earlier with the later version reveals that, though the changes made in the name of chant theory are many and significant, *most* of the changes are merely corrections of the Metz musical "dialect," thus ensuring greater conformity of the Cistercian repertory with the chant we would style "standard."

Bernard's role in the chant reform

Nothing in the *Prologus* or in other sources suggests that Bernard himself was an expert theorist or musicologist. His chief role in the reform was that of organizer and coordinator; and though this postulates, on his part, at least a basic knowledge of the chant theories implemented in the reform, this knowledge need not have been remarkably extensive or profound.

But Bernard nevertheless has something to teach us by his attitude towards music.

For those who have concerned themselves with the nature of music, there have always been two chief centers of emphasis. Many have been concerned with the *effects* of music; thus, music is envisaged first and foremost in its ethical connotations, i.e., in its function as an instrument for the promotion of the individual in good or for his debasement in evil: Plato, Aristotle, Augustine. Others have been more concerned for the structure of music as it is in itself, stressing the *essence* of music rather than its effects. For these, music is largely an affair of the reason. It is, therefore, submitted to laws, and admits of precise analyses in terms of ratios and mathematical formulae: Boethius . . . and the authors of our own Cistercian chant treatises. These latter tended to analyze the nature of music, draw up a canon of rules which music ought to follow, and then re-write the music to make it conform with the rules.

However sympathetic he was to this topic, Bernard's own references to music strike a quite different note. Nowhere does he deal so explicitly with the nature of ecclesiastical music as in the letter he wrote to Abbot Guy of Montiéramey (1137–1163), when he sent Dom Guy the St Victor Office composed by Bernard at his request. "The chant if it is employed," writes St Bernard, "should be quite solemn, nothing sensuous or rustic. Its sweetness should not be frivolous. It should please the ear only that it might move the heart, taking away sorrow and mitigating wrath. *It should not detract from the sense of the words but rather make it more fruitful.*"[5]

For Bernard, music is in the service of something higher than itself. Its function is to deepen one's experience of the life-giving word of God, to intensify the richness of one's spiritual experience. This concept of music as a "fecundation of the text" is more than interesting; it is of prime importance for our own efforts in the direction of a sung monastic office suitable for our own contemporary context.

Chrysogonus Waddell ocso

Gethsemani Abbey
   Trappist, Kentucky

---

5. *Letter* 389, PL 182:611. A full translation of this letter as well as the Office of St Victor will be found further on in this volume.

PROLOGUE TO THE CISTERCIAN
ANTIPHONARY

BERNARD, humble Abbot of Clairvaux,
To all who are to transcribe this Antiphonary, or sing from it.

THERE WERE A NUMBER of things for which our Fathers, that is to say, those who began the Cistercian Order, were zealous, and rightly so. Among these concerns, the chanting of the divine praises according to the most authentic version was the object of their most earnest, dedicated efforts. They accordingly sent persons to transcribe and bring back the Metz Antiphonary, since this Antiphonary, it was said, was "Gregorian." They found the reality far different from what they had heard. For, upon examination, the Antiphonary proved unsatisfactory: texts and melodies were found to be corrupt, quite badly structured, and deserving of contempt in almost every respect. But once they had begun, they put it into use and retained it up to our own day. The time finally came, however, when our brethren, i.e., the Abbots of our Order, were no longer able to put up with it. Having agreed that the Antiphonary was to be revised and corrected, they put me in charge of the task. I, however, summoned those of these same brethren of ours, who proved to be better instructed and more skillful in the theory and practice of chant. We put together the new Antiphonary — presented in the following volume — from many different sources; and we believe that, textually and musically, it is beyond reproach. Anyone who sings from this Antiphonary will prove this (provided, of course, he knows something about chant).

We therefore wish that, from now on, the Antiphonary as revised and contained in this volume, be adopted in our monasteries, both as regards texts and melodies; and, in virtue of the authority of the whole General Chapter, where this Antiphonary was accepted and confirmed by all the Abbots, we prohibit any change whatsoever to be made by anyone, and in any way. Should the Reader wish to know in greater detail the reasons and principles behind the present revision, he should read the following Preface, which the above-mentioned revisers of the old Antiphonary were at pains to prefix to the new version. A clear exposé of the textual and musical faults of the earlier volume will make the necessity and usefulness of the revised, corrected Antiphonary appear in clearer light.

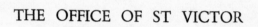

THE OFFICE OF ST VICTOR

INTRODUCTION

PERHAPS THE THING that interests us most in regard to the Office of St Victor is the covering letter which St Bernard composed when he sent this office to the Abbot and monks of Montiéramey (S Petri Arremarensis).[1] In this letter Bernard expresses concisely the qualities he believes should be found in liturgical texts and chants so that they might truly fulfill their proper function in the cultic life of the ecclesial community. On the other hand the texts of the Office itself do not offer us anything of particularly great interest save perhaps the witness to Bernard's fidelity to tradition.[2] Indeed it adheres strictly to the established form (in this undoubtedly St Bernard had no choice), but also the mode of expression and the choice of sources are wholly in line with prevailing practice. As we would expect, the Bible is the principal source employed.[3] The historical allusions are drawn largely from a *Life* of the Saint which was sent to Bernard by Abbot

---

1. A translation to this letter appears below as an appendix to this section.
2. Dom Jean Leclercq has produced an interesting study on the Office, exploring with care its Latin vocabulary: "Saint Bernard Ecrivain d'après l'Office de Saint Victor" in *Revue Bénédictine*, 74 (1964), pp. 155–169, reproduced in *Recueil d'études sur saint Bernard et ses écrits II* (Rome: Edizioni di Storia e Letteratura, 1966), pp. 149–168. Its greatest value for Leclercq seems to lie in the witness it gives to certain qualities in the author.
3. There are no direct citations, but very many allusions. For a listing of these, see Leclercq, *op. cit.*, pp. 163f.

Guy of Montiéramey.[4] The two Sermons for the Feast of St Victor[5] (which will appear in a later volume of the CISTERICAN FATHERS SERIES) which St Bernard intended to be used as the lessons at this Office also draw something from this *Life*. But Bernard, the cenobite, writing an office for a cenobitical community, generally passed over the eremitical aspects of the Saint's career. On the whole the texts are not found to be particularly inspiring, at least not in today's liturgical climate, yet they do give some taste of what was in vogue at that time and what appealed to Bernard's sense of piety. They also give an example of the structure of the office that was proper to the Benedictines at that time.[6] Whether Bernard himself composed any of the music which is found with these texts in the manuscripts is unknown.[7]

It is not possible to date the composition of this Office precisely. It was written for use at the Abbey of Montiéramey where the body of St Victor was preserved with veneration, at the insistent request of the Abbot, Guy, and his community.[8] As Guy became abbot in 1137 the Office must have been composed sometime after that date and before the death of Bernard in 1153. At Montiéramey they celebrated two feasts in honor of St Victor: his *dies natalis*, February 26th, and the translation of his relics. The Office seems to have been composed for the former feast, and was actually employed on that day.[9]

4. ". . . the ancient life of the Saint which you sent me. . . ." (St Bernard's letter to Abbot Guy). This *Life* is probably substantially the same as the one to be found in *Acta Sanctorum Boll.*, Feb. III, 3rd ed. (Paris, 1865), pp. 671f.

5. PL 183:371–376.

6. "There is also a responsory for the first vespers and, *according to your custom*, two short responsories. . . ." (St Bernard's letter to Abbot Guy). There is some indication that these might have actually been added to the Office by Bernard, after he had composed the rest, at the specific request of the Abbot; see Leclercq, *op. cit.*, pp. 150ff.

7. Leclercq raises the question but leaves it to the musicologists to solve (*op. cit.*, pp. 153f.). In publishing his study, he gives generous credit to the assistance of one of the most qualified musicologists for this period, Fr Chrysogonus Waddell OCSO.

8. "When I delay, you insist; when I make excuses, you urge me on. . . ." (St Bernard's letter to Abbot Guy).

9. Ms. Troyes 721, f. 42.

The translation presented here is based on the critical edition of the Office prepared by Dom Jean Leclercq and Henri Rochais and published in the third volume of the *S. Bernardi Opera* (Rome, 1963). In his introduction to this edition, Dom Jean Leclercq notes that there is no known manuscript that contains the entire Office as it is described by Bernard in his letter to Abbot Guy.[10] However, actually the oldest extant manuscript, Troyes 721, is also the most complete, and has largely been used as the basis of the critical edition. While the catalog ascribes this twelfth-century manuscript to Montier-la-Celle, in all probability it actually comes from Montiéramey itself.[11] While several Latin editions have appeared since it was first published in 1616 by J. Picard, a canon regular of St Victor of Paris, this is to our knowledge the first time that it has appeared in English translation.

M. Basil Pennington ocso

St Joseph's Abbey
Spencer, Massachusetts

10. "Then in regard to the singing I have composed a hymn. . . . I have arranged twelve responsories and thirty-seven antiphons, putting each in its proper place. There is also a responsory for the first vespers and, according to your custom, two short responsories for the feast, one for lauds and the other for vespers" (St Bernard's letter to Abbot Guy). The count of thirty-seven antiphons is arrived at by including the four which Bernard had prepared for the octave day. These are not included in the present translation as they are not included in the critical edition.

11. See the introduction in the critical edition: *S. Bernardi Opera*, III (Rome: Editiones Cistercienses, 1963), pp. 497f.

M

THE OFFICE OF ST VICTOR

FIRST VESPERS

First Antiphon

O victorious soul, you, like a wary sparrow, avoided the fowler's snare; we though are caught in it; come, snatch us out.

Second Antiphon

O veteran soldier, your battle is over, your deserved retirement has come; we though are still engaged amid hostile swords; come, look on us as we sing your praises.

Third Antiphon

O Victor renowned, how gloriously you triumphed over the foe; to you we belong; yours is the glory at stake if ever the foe should glory over us.

Fourth Antiphon

O victorious Jesus, yours was the victory our Victor won. Let him glory in you, but let him not forget us here.

Responsory

A Victor indeed! As long as you lived, you lifted the banner of victory in triumph after triumph from the womb to the tomb. * Your victories give us heart; may your weaponry give us security.

℣. That we be enabled to resist on the evil day, and in all things to stand perfect. * Your victories . . . ℣. Glory be to the Father and to the Son and to the Holy Spirit.

HYMN

Victor, whose life is splendid for its merit—
life here on earth, yet not of earth, not earthy;
heavenly rather, given as a model
　　for imitation.

In him was living, not himself but Jesus;
Christ in him, showing dead men ways of living,
men of this world the ways of men of heaven,
　　seeking to match them.

Men whose profession called for saintly conduct
found too in Victor model and example:
decency, honor, uncorrupted virtue,
　　integral, holy.

That is the reason why the heavens opened,
why he beheld the vision of the angels—
angels who love to show themselves to human
　　eyes that are modest.

Glory to highest Trinity of Godhead;
glory unique for three all-holy persons;
total for each and undivided singly—
　　three who are one God.

℣. Pray for us, O blessed Victor.

Magnificat Antiphon

O the magnitude of the power of your Lord, Blessed Victor, and of his kindness too! Favorable to us as he was lavish to you; powerful in you, and through you a savior for us!

VIGILS

Invitatory

Take courage; Victor has conquered the world; let us rejoice in
his victory that we too may conquer.

HYMN

Fitting it was that one still in this body,
curbing his flesh though from its fleshy longing,
living angelic, should be hearing angels
    singing so friendly.

Fitting indeed that he, the designated
Vessel of Honor, keep himself all-holy
for a vocation given him within the
    womb of his mother.

Ghosts we are told of saw his mother pregnant,
nor could withstand the presence of her infant;
fled they and named him Victor, Saint and Holy,
    closed in the womb still.

Nor did he later disappoint the hopes of
all that he promised in so ripe a childhood;
rather he added yet maturer living,
    greater in growing.

Glory to highest Trinity of Godhead;
glory unique for three all-holy persons;
total for each and undivided singly—
    three who are one God.

FIRST NOCTURN

First Antiphon

Blessed the man who loved the law and ambitioned not the
prelate's chair.

Second Antiphon

He served the Lord in fear, and now without tremor he exults
before him.

N

Third Antiphon

He walked, O Lord, in the light of your countenance, and now that light is sealed upon him.

Fourth Antiphon

Those words of yours, O Lord—Victor received them into his ears and into his heart. It was they that gave him his victory.

Fifth Antiphon

In Victor's mouth was perfect praise, for in his heart there was perpetual peace.

Sixth Antiphon

He was confident in the Lord; in vain did they try to waylay him, those who shoot from ambush on the upright of heart.

℣. The Lord loved him and adorned him.
℟. He clothed him with a robe of glory.

First Responsory

O what a man of outstanding holiness! Saint before he was born, a Victor before he was named! * Enclosed in the womb and already triumphant over the foe! ℣. Lord, you anticipated with him, and gave him in advance the choicest of blessings. * Enclosed....

Second Responsory

O what a miracle, joyous and rare! A lion roaring and in flight * from a child who has not yet cried! ℣. As wax melts and runs before fire, so do sinners perish. * From. . . .

Third Responsory

O what a mother, and how fortunate! Her womb underwent a

renewal no mother had experienced * since the days of John the Baptist! ℣. There was not found the like of him. * Since. . . .

Fourth Responsory

O good Jesus, yours is the power, yours the victory, whereby one little lamb * set a whole pack of wolves in panic. ℣. Before the child would know how to call father or mother. * Set. . . .

℣. Glory be to the Father and to the Son and to the Holy Spirit. O good. . . .

SECOND NOCTURN

Seventh Antiphon

The Malignant One was annihilated before him, that he might live up to his name of Victor.

Eighth Antiphon

Lord, in your strength will Victor rejoice, for he knows that his victory came not from his own.

Ninth Antiphon

Not in vain did he accept his soul, he who ruled his life by reason. And that is why he has been able to climb the mountain of the Lord.

Tenth Antiphon

From the fear of the enemy you have snatched, O Lord, the soul of the Saint. And now that the victory is his, no fighting remains for him.

Eleventh Antiphon

For you a hymn, for you all praise, you whose doing it was that our Victor, freed from the flesh, should be able to free a man in chains.

Twelfth Antiphon

Good it is to confess to the Lord. The merits of the saints are gifts from him. To him Saint Victor confesses his debt as being a victor.

℣. The Lord led the just man through right paths.
℞. And showed him the Kingdom of God.

Fifth Responsory
The King of the Franks, passing by the hermit's dwelling, was impressed by what was being said * of this man. ℣. So many things we have heard and learned, and our fathers have told us. * Of this man. . . .

Sixth Responsory
Rumor had already made known the hidden treasure and it could not bypass a passing king. * He therefore stopped off at the poor man's hut, enticed by the renown of his holiness. ℣. That he might see the works of the Lord, and his wonders in the desert. * He therefore. . . .

Seventh Responsory
When the king entered the impoverished cell, his host took good care of him. There was no wine, but he drew water from a nearby spring, blessed it, and turned it into wine. And so they all drank, * the King himself and his companions. ℣. All were filled with stupor and ecstasy over what had befallen him. * The King. . . .

Eighth Responsory
The waters poise in earthen jars; a new command resounds: "Be poured!" * The waters hear their Lord and blush to wine.

℣. The right hand of the Lord has wrought mightily. * The waters hear. . . . ℣. Glory be to the Father and to the Son and to the Holy Spirit. The waters poise. . . .

THIRD NOCTURN

Antiphon for the Canticles
How comforting, how pleasant, how welcome a thing it is, in

this place of affliction, in this body of death, to have you, O Victor, to sing of, you to devote ourselves to, you to implore for aid!

℣. The just man shall flourish as the palm tree.
℞. As the cedar of Lebanon shall he grow.

Ninth Responsory

A certain man, unashamed to malign the Saint, stole his wheat and hid it underground, and thereupon miserably * fell victim to a malignant spirit. ℣. Cursed be the man who hides corn from the people. * He fell. . . .

Tenth Responsory

A miracle sad but just! * The man who bore with the demon while he suggested the crime had to bear with him also while he avenged it! ℣. You are just, O Lord, and your award is right. * The man. . . .

Eleventh Responsory

What a revelation of the mysteries of iniquity! A demon prompts a man; the man exposes the demon; Victor steps in and arbitrates between the two. * He routs the demon, heals the man, and gets his wheat back in return. Wickedness indeed will out! ℣. The Lord was with him amid the fraud of those who tried to outsmart him, and he kept him honorable. * He routs. . . .

Twelfth Responsory

Victor looked upwards and saw the heavens opened and a cross adorned with jewels. A voice came to him: "The jewels are souls; * they have reached a share in the glory of the Cross for having borne its ignominy." ℣. Let Israel rejoice in him that made him, and the daughters of Sion rejoice in their King. * They have. . . .

℣. Glory be to the Father and to the Son and to the Holy Spirit. Victor. . . .

LAUDS

First Antiphon

Victor's body dwelt on earth; his mind in heaven, where it heard angelic voices, sometimes carrying a message, sometimes waxing ineffable in melodious song.

Second Antiphon

He has now entered the heavens which he used to see opened before his blessed eyes. Now indeed he beholds unveiled the face of God in glory.

Third Antiphon

Blessed is that vision whereby you, O Victor, are transformed into the selfsame image, from brightness to brightness, as by the Spirit of the Lord.

Fourth Antiphon

O Victor, you once beheld a Cross studded with gems; one of the gems is your soul. For your soul was truly encrusted into the Cross, along with the inlaid jewelry of Divine Glory, the image of whose splendor you now are wearing.

Fifth Antiphon

Almighty Father, we have sinned against you and become alienated as your sons. Let our Victor, who conquered his own covetousness, conquer your wrath and bring us back to you, restoring us mightily to your grace.

Responsory

Daughters of Jerusalem, a holy soul is taking leave of earth; * go forth now and meet it. ℣. Coming it shall come with exultation. * Go forth. . . . ℣. Glory be to the Father and to the Son and to the Holy Spirit. Daughters. . . .

HYMN

Wine from a flowing fountain, not a grape-vine;
water from springs that don a richer color,
bless'd by a sign from Blessed Victor's fingers
    used as a wine-press.
Color and taste and all that wine is made of
enter the limpid waters and renew them,
leave there the royal party standing speechless,
    royally drinking.
Tortured by demons, guilty too of thieving,
yet could he never hide himself from Victor.
Out goes that cruel torturer to suffer
    torture himself now.
Such is sufficient proof amid so many
signs of the glory Victor won of sainthood,
signs of the Spirit dwelling deep within him,
    teaching him goodness.
Glory to highest Trinity of Godhead;
glory unique for three all-holy persons;
total for each and undivided singly—
    three who are one God.

℣. Pray for us, O Blessed Victor.

Benedictus Antiphon

How fortunate the generation for whom Victor arose as a light
in the dark, to shine on those who sat in darkness and the shadow
of death.

PRIME

Antiphon

Today Victor has put aside the body which alone stood between
him and his entry into glory. Rich in merits, glorious in signs, how
speedily he penetrates into the holy realms, transformed and glorious
like the saints.

TERCE

Antiphon

Your name and your memory, O Victor, are as dripping honeycomb to the lips of us captives here. Come then, O sturdy athlete, friendly patron, faithful advocate; rise up and help us, that you may glory in the fullness of your victory.

SEXT

Antiphon

In his victory, God made room for him upon his bosom, just as in battle he had lent him his spirit. Now that he is with you, O God, who are everywhere, do you inspire him to think of us miserable creatures. Accept him as he supplicates for us. Give him a hearing as he pleads for us, O God.

NONE

Antiphon

Victor has been swallowed up into glory. O Son of God, make him ever mindful of us; let him take up and defend our cause in your own dread judgment.

SECOND VESPERS

First Antiphon

Holy Victor, who could worthily tell your praises, the luster of your chastity, the strength of your mind, the purity of your conscience?

Second Antiphon

Holy Victor, who will enable us to abide in the memory of your abundant kindness and the goodness of your life?

Third Antiphon

Holy Victor, send us help from the Holy Realm, and from Sion protect us, even as we send praise to you from the earth.

Fourth Antiphon

Holy Victor, your holiness and your victory are as glorious to you as they are salutary to us.

Responsory

Behold the Victor, arriving full glorious. * Come, hasten to bring the crown. ℣. Now he is entering into the joy of his Lord. * Come. . . . ℣. Glory be to the Father and to the Son and to the Holy Spirit. Behold. . . .

Magnificat Antiphon

O magnificent Victor, although your magnificence rises higher than the heavens, your constant munificence does not abandon the needy of the earth.

APPENDIX

St Bernard's Letter to Abbot Guy and the Monks of Montiéramey[1]
  To Guy, the venerable Abbot of Montiéramey,
  and the holy Brothers who are with him,
  from Bernard, their servant,
  that they might serve the Lord in holiness.

You ask me, my dearest Abbot Guy, and at the same time all your Brothers who are with you, that I write for you an office which you can solemnly recite or sing on the Feast of St Victor, whose sacred relics are preserved in your midst. When I delay, you insist; when I make excuses, you urge me on, ignoring my embarrassment, even though it is fully justified. You enlist others to join in your request, as if anything could incline me to your will more cogently than your own desires. But indeed in considering this matter you ought to think not of your affection for me but rather of my place in the Church. In a matter of such importance it is not a friend that you are looking for but one who is learned and worthy, whose authority is greater, whose life is holier, whose style is more developed and whose work shows forth and is in keeping with true holiness.

Should the writings of one who is so insignificant among the people of God be read in the Churches? How little is my genius

---

1. As the critical edition of the Letters of St Bernard is not yet complete, this translation is based on Mabillon's edition found in Migne: PL 182:609–612.

and eloquence that one should single me out to ask for texts of celebration and praise. What is this? Should I now here on earth begin a new hymn of praise for him whom the heavens already hold to be praiseworthy and glorified? To want to add something to the heavenly praises is to detract from them. Not that men should fail to praise one who has been glorified by the angels, but in their celebrations anything savoring of novelty or frivolity would be out of place. There is room here only for the authentic and the traditional which edifies the Church and bears the stamp of her dignity. If something new is to be heard, because the situation requires it, I believe, as I have said, those things are to be used which will please the hearts of the hearers and be useful to them because of the dignity both of the expression and of the author. Furthermore, the texts must be clear, shining forth with unclouded truth, proclaiming justice, urging humility, teaching equity. They should bring forth truth in our minds, virtue in our action; crucify our vices, inflame devotion, and discipline our senses. The chant if it is employed should be quite solemn, nothing sensuous or rustic. Its sweetness should not be frivolous. It should please the ear only that it might move the heart, taking away sorrow and mitigating wrath. It should not detract from the sense of the words, but rather make it more fruitful. It is not a little blow to spiritual profit when more attention is paid to feats of voice than to the meaning of words.

This then is what ought to be heard in the Church and the kind of man the author ought to be. Am I such a man, and have I ever composed such things? And nevertheless you come pounding on the door of my poverty, arousing me. If not because of your friendship, certainly because of your importunity, I have risen, according to the word of the Lord, to give you what you have demanded (Lk 11:8). I have given you not what you really wanted, but what has come to my hand; what I could manage, and not what you wished. Basing myself on the facts found in the ancient Life of the Saint which you sent me, I have dictated two sermons, using my own mode of expression. I have tried not to be tiresomely long. Then in regard to the singing I have composed a hymn in which I have sacrificed the meter in order that the meaning might stand out better. I have arranged twelve responsories and twenty-seven antiphons,[2] putting each in its proper place. There is also a responsory for the first vespers and, according to your custom, two short responsories for the feast, one for lauds and the other for vespers. For all this I demand my pay. I will not be without my reward. So what? Whether you are pleased with it or not, that matters little to me, for I have given you what I have. Therefore, give me my pay: your prayers.

2. "Twenty-seven" is the reading in Mabillon, but the more common reading of "thirty-seven" would seem to be the correct one. See Introduction, above, note 10. There are also manuscripts which read "thirty-four"; see Leclercq, *op. cit.*, p. 150.

SELECTED BIBLIOGRAPHY

1. General Works

——*Bernard de Clairvaux* (Paris: Commission d'Histoire de l'Ordre de Cîteaux, 1953).

——*S. Bernard et son temps*, 2 vols. (Dijon: l'Académie des Sciences, Artes et Belles-lettres, 1929).

——*Théologie de la vie monastique* (Paris: Aubier, 1961).

——*L'Art Cistercien* (Cahiers de la Pierre-qui-Vire, No. 16, 1962).

Bouyer, L., *The Cistercian Heritage* (London: Mowbrays, 1958).

Constable, G. and Kritzeck, J., *Petrus Venerabilis, 1156-1956* (Rome: *Studia Anselmiana*, No. 40, 1956).

Evans, Joan, *Monastic Life at Cluny 910-1157* (Oxford University Press, 1931).
,,   *Life in Mediaeval France* (Oxford University Press, 1925).

Gilson, E., *The Mystical Theology of St. Bernard* (London: Sheed & Ward, 1955).

Leclercq, J., *Pierre le vénérable* (Abbaye S. Wandrille: Editions de Fontenelle, 1946).
,,   *Etudes sur s. Bernard et le texte de ses écrits* (Rome: *Analecta S.O.C.*, fasc. 1-2, 1953).
,, (ed.) *Saint Bernard Théologien* (Rome: *Analecta S.O.C.*, fasc. 3-4, 1953).
,, (et al.) *La spiritualité du moyen âge* (Paris: Aubier, 1961).
,,   *The Love of Learning and the Desire for God* (New York: Fordham University Press, 1961; Mentor, 1962).
,,   *Aux sources de la spiritualité occidentale* (Paris: Cerf, 1964).
,,   *Témoins de la spiritualité occidentale* (Paris: Cerf, 1965).
,,   *Chances de la spiritualité occidentale* (Paris: Cerf, 1966).
,,   *Recueil d'études sur S. Bernard et ses écrits*, 3 vols. (Rome: Edizioni di Storia e Letteratura, 1962, 1966, 1969).
,,   "Les intentions des fondateurs de l'Ordre cistercien" (*Colletanea Cisterciensia*, 30 (1968), pp. 233-271).

Lekai, L. *The White Monks* (Okauchee, Wisconsin: Cistercian Fathers, 1953).

Luddy, A., *The Life and Teaching of St. Bernard* (Dublin: Gill, 1927).

Salmon, P., "Monastic Asceticism and the origins of Cîteaux" (*Monastic Studies*, No. 3, pp. 119–139).

Williams, W., *St Bernard of Clairvaux* (Manchester University Press, 1953).

2. The Cluniac-Cistercian Controversy

a) Primary Sources

Bernard's letter to Robert of Chatillion (*Ep.* I; PL 67–79; trans. James, pp. 1–10).

Peter the Venerable's letter to Bernard (Ep. I, 28; PL 112–115).

Bernard's *Apologia*.

Matthew of Albano's letter to the Benedictine Abbots of Rheims (U. Berliere, *Documents inédits pour servir a l'histoire ecclésiastique de la Belgique*, I [1894], pp. 93–110).

Peter the Venerable's *Statutes* (PL 1025–1048).

Peter the Venerable's second letter to Bernard (Ep. IV, 17; PL 321–344).

The anonymous *Dialogus inter Cluniacensem Monachum et Cisterciensem de Diversis Utrusque Ordinis Observantiis* (ed. Martène and Durand, *Thesaurus Novorum Anecdotorum*, V, col. 1569–1654).

Walter Map's "De Claravallensibus et Cluniacensibus" (ed. T. Wright, *The Latin Poems commonly attributed to Walter Mapes* [London: Camden Society, 1841]).

Hugh of Reading's *Riposte* (ed. A. Wilmart in *Revue bénédictine*, 46 [1934], pp. 309–344. Further details on all the above works are furnished by Dom Wilmart in the same article, pp. 296–309).

A monk of Bonnevaux, *Vita Amadaei*, ch. V (ed. A. Dimier in "Un témoin tardif peu connu du conflit entre cisterciens et clunisiens" in *Petrus Venerabilis, 1156–1956*, pp. 91–94).

The anonymous "Vision of a Cistercian Novice" (ed. G. Constable in *Petrus Venerabilis, 1156–1956*, pp. 96–98).

An unknown abbot's *Tractulus* (ed. J. Leclercq, "Nouvelle réponse de l'ancien monachisme aux critiques des cisterciens" in *Recueil*, II, pp. 75–85).

b) Secondary Sources

Bishop, E., "Cluniacs and Cistercians" in *The Downside Review*, 52 (1934), pp. 223–230.

Bredero, A., "The Controversy between Peter the Venerable and St Bernard of Clairvaux" in *Petrus Venerabilis, 1156–1956*, pp. 53–71.

Cabrol, F., "Cluny et Cîteaux" in *S. Bernard et son temps*, I, pp. 19–28.

Knowles, D., *Cistercians and Cluniacs* (Oxford University Press, 1955).

,,   "The Reforming Decrees of Peter the Venerable" in *Petrus Venerabilis, 1156–1956*, pp. 1–20.

,,   "Peter the Venerable" in *The Bulletin of the John Ryland's Library*, 39 (1956), pp. 132–145.

Leclercq. J., "Pierre le vénérable et les limites du programme cistercien" in *Collectanea OCR*, 17 (1956), pp. 84–87.

Talbot, C. H., "The Date and Author of the Riposte" in *Petrus Venerabilis, 1156-1956*, pp. 72–80.

Williams, W., "Peter the Venerable: a Letter to St Bernard" in *The Downside Review*, 56 (1938), pp. 344–353.

ANALYTIC INDEX

The following abbreviations are used: *apo*=Apologia; *ep*=St Bernard's Letter to Abbot Guy and the Monks of Montiéramey; *ov*=The Office of St Victor; *pre*=On Precept and Dispensation; *pro*=Prologue to the Cistercian Antiphonary. The numbers refer to the paragraphs in the texts.

Abbot, *pre* 29: irregular, *pre* 56; subject to the Rule, *pre* 9f.; witness of profession, *pre* 55; *see* dispensation.

Abstinence, *apo* 16: abuses *apo* 20ff.; example of the Fathers, *apo* 19; meat and wine good in themselves, *apo* 12; not as important as humility, *apo* 12.

Angel: spoke to St Victor, *ov*.

Anger, *pre* 56, 58.

Anthony (St), *apo* 19, 23.

Augustine (St), *pre* 2, 4, 10, 52.

Authority: abuse of, *pre* 22; divine and human, *pre* 19, 22; *see* abbot, dispensation, superiors.

Basil (St), *apo* 23; *pre* 4, 10.

Benedict (St), *pre* 3, 16, 29, 49, 55.

Benedictine Order: *see* Cluniacs.

Bernard (St); abbot of Clairvaux, *pre*, pref., *pro*; personal relations with the Cluniacs, *apo* 4, 7; protestations of humility, *ep*, *pre*, pref.; vocation, *apo* 7f.

Body, *pre* 59f.

Chant, *ep*, *pro*.

Charity: above the Rule, *pre* 9; end of the Rule, *pre* 5; necessary for the simple eye, *pre* 36; one and many, *apo* 7; *see* love.

Christ, *pre* 29, 41, 61: example, *pre* 12, 20; Savior, *apo* 5f., 19, *ov*, *pre* 24; Spouse of the Church, *apo* 6f.; sweet yoke of, *pre* 31; Truth, *apo* 16, *pre* 18, 25, 31, 35, 36, 40, 41, 56.

Church: liturgy for her edification, *ep*; spouse of Christ, *apo* 6f.; unity in variety, *apo* 6f., 8.

186

Silence, *apo* 16, *pre* 17f., 30.

Simplicity, *pre* 36; *see* intention.

Sin, *pre* 25: all offend, *pre* 24, 32, 33; mortal, *pre* 26, 33; of neglect, *pre* 18; proportionate to matter, *pre* 15, 25f., 32f.; venial, *pre* 26.

Singing, *ep*, *pro*.

Slackness, *apo* 19; causes of, *apo* 18.

Stability (local), *pre* 44ff., 55f.: everyone should remain in the vocation to which he is called, *apo* 7, 30f.; licit change, *pre* 49; subordinate to other vows, *pre* 44.

Superiors, *pre* 13: negligences of, *apo* 27; only as minister of God, *pre* 19, 21 f., 32; power to dispense, *pre* 4f.

Truth: *see* Christ, intention.

Unity: consists of singleness of love, *apo* 8; in the Church, *apo* 6ff.; manifold unity of heaven, *apo* 8; with variety, *apo* 6ff.

Victor (St), *ep*, *ov*: miracles, *ov*.

Work: relative value of manual labor, *apo* 12f.

CISTERCIAN STUDIES SERIES

Under the direction of the same Board of Editors as the CISTERCIAN FATHERS SERIES, the CISTERCIAN STUDIES SERIES seeks to make available to the English-speaking world significant studies produced in other languages, as well as various monastic texts and studies of perennial value, with a view to placing the Cistercian Fathers in their full historical context and bringing out their present-day relevance.

Cistercian Publications Spencer Massachusetts 01562
Irish University Press Shannon Ireland